Institutions on the Edge

Why does institutional instability pervade the developing world? Examining contemporary Latin America, *Institutions on the Edge* develops and tests a novel argument to explain why institutional crises emerge, spread, and repeat in some countries, but not in others. The book draws on formal bargaining theories developed in the conflict literature to offer the first unified micro-level account of inter-branch crises. In so doing, Helmke shows that concentrating power in the executive branch not only fuels presidential crises under divided government, but also triggers broader constitutional crises that cascade onto the legislature and the judiciary. Along the way, Helmke highlights the importance of public opinion and mass protests, and elucidates the conditions under which divided government matters for institutional instability.

Gretchen Helmke is Professor of Political Science at the University of Rochester. She received her Ph.D. from the University of Chicago.

Cambridge Studies in Comparative Politics

General Editor

Margaret Levi   *University of Washington, Seattle*

Assistant General Editors

Kathleen Thelen   *Massachusetts Institute of Technology*
Erik Wibbels   *Duke University*

Associate Editors

Robert H. Bates   *Harvard University*
Stephen Hanson   *University of Washington, Seattle*
Torben Iversen   *Harvard University*
Stathis Kalyvas   *Yale University*
Peter Lange   *Duke University*
Helen Milner   *Princeton University*
Frances Rosenbluth   *Yale University*
Susan Stokes   *Yale University*
Sidney Tarrow   *Cornell University*

Other Books in the Series

Christopher Adolph, *Bankers, Bureaucrats, and Central Bank Politics: The Myth of Neutrality*
Michael Albertus, *Autocracy and Redistribution: The Politics of Land Reform*
Ben W. Ansell, *From the Ballot to the Blackboard: The Redistributive Political Economy of Education*
Ben W. Ansell, David J. Samuels, *Inequality and Democratization: An Elite-Competition Approach*
Leonardo R. Arriola, *Multi-Ethnic Coalitions in Africa: Business Financing of Opposition Election Campaigns*
David Austen-Smith, Jeffry A. Frieden, Miriam A. Golden, Karl Ove Moene, and Adam Przeworski, eds., *Selected Works of Michael Wallerstein: The Political Economy of Inequality, Unions, and Social Democracy*
Andy Baker, *The Market and the Masses in Latin America: Policy Reform and Consumption in Liberalizing Economies*

Continued after the index

Institutions on the Edge

The Origins and Consequences of Inter-Branch Crises in Latin America

GRETCHEN HELMKE

University of Rochester

CAMBRIDGE
UNIVERSITY PRESS

CAMBRIDGE
UNIVERSITY PRESS

University Printing House, Cambridge CB2 8BS, United Kingdom

One Liberty Plaza, 20th Floor, New York, NY 10006, USA

477 Williamstown Road, Port Melbourne, VIC 3207, Australia

4843/24, 2nd Floor, Ansari Road, Daryaganj, Delhi – 110002, India

79 Anson Road, #06–04/06, Singapore 079906

Cambridge University Press is part of the University of Cambridge.

It furthers the University's mission by disseminating knowledge in the pursuit of education, learning, and research at the highest international levels of excellence.

www.cambridge.org
Information on this title: www.cambridge.org/9780521496148

© Gretchen Helmke 2017

First published 2017

Printed in the United States of America by Sheridan Books, Inc.

A catalogue record for this publication is available from the British Library.

Library of Congress Cataloging-in-Publication Data
NAMES: Helmke, Gretchen, 1967– author.
TITLE: Institutions on the edge : the origins and consequences of inter-branch crises in Latin America / Gretchen Helmke, University of Rochester.
DESCRIPTION: Cambridge, United Kingdom ; New York, NY : Cambridge University Press, 2017. | Includes bibliographical references and index.
IDENTIFIERS: LCCN 2016035549 | ISBN 9780521496148 (hardback) | ISBN 9780521738408 (paperback)
SUBJECTS: LCSH: Political stability–Latin America. | Executive-legislative relations–Latin America. | Divided government–Latin America. | Public opinion–Political aspects–Latin America. | Latin America–Politics and government. | BISAC: POLITICAL SCIENCE / General.
CLASSIFICATION: LCC JL960 .H46 2017 | DDC 320.98–dc23 LC record available at https://lccn.loc.gov/2016035549

ISBN 978-0-521-49614-8 Hardback
ISBN 978-0-521-73840-8 Paperback

To Rose

Contents

Figures

Tables

Preface and Acknowledgments

Many second books are inspired by questions raised by first books. This one is no exception. In studying how institutional instability constrained judicial decision-making, I became deeply interested in why instability itself emerges. Coincidentally, as I began to ponder this question, Argentina entered into a kind of institutional free fall. At the end of 2001, President De la Rúa resigned from office. With the country convulsed in economic crisis, four interim presidents followed in the space of less than a month. The next year, the new interim government, led by Eduardo Duhalde, went after the Supreme Court, seeking to impeach all nine justices on a variety of charges based on misconduct in cases ranging from the acquittal of former President Carlos Menem on corruption charges to the current government's attempts to freeze savings accounts to preserve the country's banking system. Although the Court survived this attempt, the majority of justices were ultimately impeached at the end of 2003 under Néstor Kirchner's new administration. Why inter-branch crises rage in some Latin American countries, but not in others, struck me as a fundamentally important, if underexamined, question. Because the literatures on judicial independence, presidential crises, and constitutional coups have developed along parallel tracks, no study has yet offered a unified theoretical framework explaining why, when, and how crises across branches are interrelated. This book is an attempt to fill that gap.

This book simply would not have been possible without the incredible efforts and patience of my research assistants. At the beginning of the project, Laurin Frisina, Blake Graham, Subhasish Ray, and I spent countless hours in the Fenno Room coding *Latin American Weekly Reports*. Laurin remained my research assistant, carefully cleaning and merging multiple versions of the Inter-Branch Crises in Latin America (ICLA) dataset. During the course of writing the book, Laurin tragically passed away; she is deeply missed. I am also indebted to Shawn Ling Ramirez, who helped bring me up to speed on the formal bargaining conflict literature and who provided invaluable advice and assistance for testing the theoretical framework. Kerim Kavakli and David Carter subsequently helped with the R-code that allowed me to estimate a strategic model, which was published as an article in the *American Journal of Political Science*. During the revisions stage, chronic health issues prevented me from being able to type. As a result, the entire manuscript has been written via dictation with the help of three people: Rabia Malik, Yeon-Kyung Jeong, and Grace Grande. Although challenging, this process has made writing far less isolating and much more fun. I cannot express deeply enough my gratitude for their support, patience, and insights.

Field work for this project was carried out in Ecuador during the summer of 2008. Santiago Basabe was an outstanding host and research assistant. I am very grateful to the following politicians, judges, academics, and journalists for taking the time to meet with me and to share their views on institutional instability: President of the Constituent Assembly Alberto Acosta, President Fabián Alarcón, President Rosalia Arteaga, Minister of Foreign Relations José Ayala-Lasso, Deputy Raúl Baca Carbo, President Rodrigo Borja, Deputy Diego Delgado, Thalia Flores, Professor Agustín Grijalva, President Lucio Gutiérrez, José Hernández, Justice Minister Gustavo Jahlk, Deputy Wilfrido Lucero, General Pablo Moncayo, Professor César Montúfar, President Gustavo Naboa, Deputy Diego Ordoñez, Professor Simón Pachano, Deputy Andrés Páez, Deputy Marco Proano, Secretary of Education René Ramírez Gallegos, Miguel Rivadeneira, Judge Hernán Salgado, Justice Carlos Solorzano, Deputy Alexandra Vela, Justice José Vicente Troya, and Justice Alberto Wray.

Early versions of this project were presented at the Annual Meeting of the Political Science Association, Chicago, IL, August 2006; the Law and Political Economy Workshop at the Northwestern University Law School; the Annual Meeting of the Midwest Political Science Association, Chicago, IL, April 2007; the Latin American Discussion Group at Harvard, October 2009; and the Woodrow Wilson Center, Washington, DC, 2011. For comments and suggestions on the project, I am extremely grateful to Kevin Clarke, Ethan Bueno de Mesquita, Jorge Dominguez, Lee Epstein, Barbara Geddes, Steve Levitsky, Aníbal Pérez-Liñán, Mitch Sanders, Curt Signorino, Susan Stokes, and Chris Zorn. Hein Goemans and Bing Powell were kind enough to read the entire manuscript.

The first draft of this book was written during a year-long sabbatical at the Woodrow Wilson Center in Washington, DC. During my time there, I benefited enormously from conversations with Larry Altman, Cynthia Arnson, Donald Horowitz, and Joseph Sassoon. Johnnie Lotesta provided excellent research assistance. Parts of Chapter 3 were published in the *American Journal of Political Science* under the title, "The Origins of Institutional Crises in Latin America." Parts of Chapter 7 were published in *Journal of Constitutional Law*, titled "Public Support and Judicial Crises in Latin America."

I could not have written this book without the encouragement of my friends and family. The following women, in particular, provided a constant source of inspiration and much needed laughter: Stephanie Dennis, Gretchen Keyes, Bonnie Meguid, Kristin Nastav, Lynda Powell, Tziporah Rosenberg, Liz Ross, Carmen Signorino, Renee Smith, Jo-anne Tartaglia, and Tracy Taurmina. I am also very grateful to my father, Stephen, my stepmother, Linda, my in-laws, Karen & Barry, my aunt Jan, and my cousin, Fran, for all of their love and support. Most especially, I want to thank my husband, Mitch, for his wisdom, strength, kindness, and unfailing sense of humor. In the middle of writing this book, we adopted our amazing daughter, Rose. Rose makes every challenge easier, every achievement sweeter, every day better. This book is dedicated to her.

I

Introduction

Institutional crises pervade the developing world. Nowhere is this more apparent than contemporary Latin America, a region notorious for failed presidents, heavily politicized courts, and legislatures that have either been summarily closed or effectively superseded. Although democratic regimes have largely endured over the last three and half decades, many of the region's main institutional actors have not. Since the third wave of democratic transitions began, nearly twenty elected Latin American leaders have been forced out of office early.[1] The list ranges from presidents elected in the 1980s, such as Bolivia's Hernán Siles Zuazo, who found his mandate cut short in the midst of major economic crises, to the seemingly textbook impeachments carried out against Presidents Fernando Collor de Melo in Brazil and Carlos Andrés Pérez in Venezuela during the 1990s to the more recent and controversial ousters of other democratically elected leaders such as Manuel Zelaya in Honduras in 2009, Fernando Lugo in Paraguay in 2012, Otto Pérez Molina in Guatemala in 2015, and Dilma Rousseff in 2016. As this book goes to press, the Venezuelan opposition is seeking signatures to remove Hugo Chávez's successor, President Nicolás Maduro.

Meanwhile, during the same period scores of judges on high courts throughout Central and South America have been sacked or had their

[1] Argentina 1989, 2001; Bolivia 1985, 2003; Brazil 1992, 2016; Dominican Republic 1996; Ecuador 1997, 2002, 2005; Guatemala 1993, 2015; Honduras 2009; Paraguay 1999, 2012; Peru 2000; Venezuela 1993. In addition, in the following countries interim presidents have been removed: Argentina 2001, 2002 (2); Bolivia 2005; Brazil 1987.

benches stacked – often repeatedly. Carlos Menem's packing of the Argentine Supreme Court during the early 1990s quickly comes to mind. As do the multiple attempts by his opponents to "reverse the damage," which eventually succeeded under Néstor Kirchner a decade later. Likewise, the longstanding control exercised over Ecuador's Supreme Court by the Partido Social Cristiano (PSC), led for years by León Febres Cordero, ultimately fed into Lucio Gutiérrez's spectacularly ill-fated effort to remake the courts in 2005. In Bolivia, Evo Morales' repeated recent attempts to purge the judiciary resulted in the wholly untenable situation in which only a single justice, Silvia Salame Farjat, sat on the Constitutional Tribunal between 2007 and 2009. Similarly egregious attacks on national high courts have been carried out in Peru, Venezuela, Paraguay, and Nicaragua.

Nor have legislatures remained entirely unscathed. Although Latin American congresses have been subjected to institutional instability far less frequently than the other two main branches of government, their survival has also been called into question, particularly in the Andean countries. The signal case here is the *autogolpe* (self-coup) carried out by Alberto Fujimori in Peru in 1992, in which the president used tanks to surround and shut down Congress. A year later, Guatemala's president, Jorge Serrano Elías, tried and failed to do the same. More recently, leaders such as Hugo Chávez in Venezuela and Rafael Correa in Ecuador have instead relied on constituent assemblies controlled by the president's supporters to do their dirty work.

That inter-branch crises, which I treat throughout the book as the attempt by one branch of government to remove or otherwise take control over another branch of government, are now primarily the purview of civilian politicians rather than generals offers only partial consolation. Throughout the region, such crises are widely blamed for short-circuiting elections, undermining faith in existing institutions, and threatening investor confidence and economic growth. According to many observers, the widespread failure of institutions in the region is one of the most important and difficult challenges facing citizens and policy makers alike today. Noting the relative absence of the military in contemporary Latin American politics, former US Assistant Secretary of State for the Western Hemisphere Arturo Valenzuela lamented,

The ratcheting down of polarization and the military's withdrawal to the barracks have not, however, ushered in an era of uniformly successful presidential governments. Instability remains a persistent problem.

(Valenzuela, 2004: 5–6)

And yet it is just as tempting to conclude that such instability may not be that problematic after all. If corrupt presidents or crooked judges are being impeached for their misdeeds, then shouldn't we instead simply infer that checks and balances are working properly? To cite an easy example, it is hard to dispute that the quality of democracy in the Dominican Republic was vastly improved by forcing fraudulently elected President Joaquín Balaguer to leave office early. Likewise, imagine how experts would have reacted had Fernando Collor de Mello not been impeached following revelations about the corruption endemic in his administration. Or consider recent events in Guatemala. Caught in the middle of a corruption scandal uncovered by the International Commission against Impunity (CICIG), pundits have applauded the stunning resignation of Guatemalan president Otto Pérez Molina, touting his downfall as a sign of a "democratic spring" in Central America.[2] More broadly, considering that one of the longstanding concerns about presidentialism in Latin America is its rigidity, and, hence, its vulnerability to regime breakdown, presidential crises might well be taken as a positive sign that these systems are adopting "parliamentary traits" (Carey, 2005; Pérez-Liñán, 2005, 2007; Marsteintredet and Berntzen, 2008).

Notwithstanding these important observations, there are at least two reasons why we should remain skeptical. First, as Chapter 2 will discuss in greater detail, in the vast majority of these instances the resolutions to such inter-branch crises have hardly been politically neutral. One branch can always generate seemingly valid reasons for going after another, but when we look closely at the process of succession and replacement it is hard to escape the conclusion that such actions primarily serve as partisan tools. Latin American presidents are famous for decrying the politicization and corruption of the courts and legislatures only to reconstitute them with their own loyal supporters. Likewise, legislatures are often all too quick to bypass vice presidents and replace ousted leaders with members of the opposition. Second, in line with the more general theoretical arguments developed below, it remains the case that checks and balances are designed primarily to serve as a deterrent. Thus, even if presidents who committed misdeeds are appropriately removed from office, we should still be concerned that institutions are failing ex ante, at least in this basic sense.

---

[2] *BBC Monitoring Latin America*, September 7, 2015.

Of course, even a casual glance at contemporary Latin American history shows that such institutional instability does not plague all countries or institutions equally. Since the 1980s, presidents have been routinely forced from power in Ecuador and Bolivia, but never in Chile, nor in Mexico. Legislatures have been closed in Peru and Venezuela, but not in Argentina or Brazil. Judges have been impeached in Argentina, Venezuela, Peru, and Bolivia, but have been allowed to remain relatively independent in Uruguay, Costa Rica, and Brazil. This variation provides the overarching empirical puzzle that motivates this book. Why do only certain countries get caught in instability traps, while others manage conflict in more "normal" ways? If some political actors in the region routinely fail to avert conflicts that threaten each other's very survival, why do others succeed? Do the same factors that spawn a crisis in one branch of government spill over into other branches? And, if so, why, when, and how?

In seeking to answer these questions, this book contributes to a long and distinguished line of scholarship in comparative politics that focuses on problems of institutional instability and weakness in the developing world (e.g., Diamond and Linz, 1989; O'Donnell, 1994; Domínguez and Shifter, 2003). Scholars of Latin American politics, in particular, have made considerable headway over the last two decades in showing how different institutional configurations affect both regime stability (Linz, 1990, 1994; Mainwaring and Shugart, 1997; Cheibub, 2007) and the prospects for democratic consolidation (e.g., see Hagopian and Mainwaring, 2005). Along the way, academics and pundits alike have bemoaned both the inability of the region's presidents to complete their terms and the frequency with which presidents meddle with legislatures and courts. However, aside from a growing number of empirical studies on presidential removals in Latin America and elsewhere (Carey, 2003; Valenzuela, 2004; Lehoucq, 2005; Mainwaring and Pérez-Liñán, 2005; Hochstetler, 2006; Negretto, 2006; Pérez-Liñán, 2007; Kim and Bahry, 2008; Hochstetler and Edwards, 2009; Llanos and Marsteintredet, 2010), systematic explanations of how and why inter-branch crises originate across all three branches of government are in short supply.

I aim to fill this gap by developing the novel intuition that inter-branch crises are theoretically analogous to inter-state wars. Leaving aside the rather obvious fact that domestic actors do not necessarily fight over territory nor suffer battle deaths, I shall argue that inter-branch crises ultimately pose the same theoretical puzzle that inter-state wars do. That is, assuming that political actors are rational – or at least boundedly so – and that inter-branch conflicts are potentially costly and risky, such crises beg the fundamental question of why institutional actors fail to resolve their disputes through negotiation and compromise. To paraphrase Fearon (1995), inter-branch crises compel us to understand why certain domestic political actors fail to strike deals with each other that both would prefer to a costly institutional fight.

The answers that I explore in the rest of this book are rooted in the familiar problems associated with asymmetric information and the inability to make credible commitments. These mechanisms have been extensively developed in the formal theoretical literature in international relations to explain the emergence of war (Fearon, 1995, 1998; Powell, 1999, 2002; Wagner, 2000; Smith and Stam, 2006; Wittman, 2009; Fey and Ramsay, 2011). Here, I apply informally the insights provided by existing game theoretical models to illuminate why some domestic actors fall prey to inter-branch crises and others manage to avoid it. In so doing, I not only supply the micro-foundations for several familiar arguments about the importance of minority governments, social protests, and presidential powers, I also provide new insights into why certain types of institutional configurations lead to failure and how different types of inter-branch crises – presidential, legislative, and judicial – are fundamentally linked to one another.

1.1 THE LITERATURE

Inter-branch crises in presidentialist systems that rise to the level of one branch threatening the constitution of another are a conundrum for classic and contemporary theories of democratic institutions. Described in *Federalist 51* (Hamilton, Madison, and Jay, 1961 [1788]), America's founding fathers conceived of a system in which granting overlapping powers to the other branches of government serves as the primary means of keeping each branch in its place. Dispelling the notion that the Constitution of the United States was based on a pure separation of powers (SOP), Bernard Manin emphasizes that the system of checks and balances advocated by Publius was designed to create a self-enforcing equilibrium in which

... each [branch] would be discouraged from encroaching upon the jurisdiction of another by the fear of retaliation and the prospective costs of such an encroachment.

(Manin, 1989: 57)

Interestingly, however, *Federalist 51* makes no mention of the main sanctioning tool used to permanently remove actors in another branch of government: impeachment. Madison's several "auxiliary precautions" designed to prevent the concentration of power in any one branch of government range from dividing legislative powers between the House and Senate to providing the executive with a legislative veto to erecting a federal government, which serves to multiply the interests of citizens and thus diminishes the likelihood of oppressive majorities forming. Within the most famous treatise on checks and balances, however, there is not a single reference to the legislature's capacity to remove either the president or the judiciary. Discussions of impeachment – and often only very brief discussions at that – are instead relegated to subsequent papers dealing with the specific powers of the Senate (*Federalist 64* and *65*) and the judiciary (*Federalist 78* and *81*).

Yet clearly the founding fathers viewed impeachment as a powerful legislative tool for preventing tyranny, as well as a power that could be misused for partisan or personal gain. With respect to the Senate's power to remove the executive, Hamilton warns,

A well constituted court for the trial of impeachments is an object not more to be desired than difficult to be obtained in a government wholly elective ... In many cases it will connect itself with the preexisting factions, and will enlist all their animosities, partialities, influence and interest on one side or the other; and in such cases there will always be the greatest danger that the decision will be regulated more by the comparative strength of parties, than by the real demonstrations of innocence or guilt.

(1961 [1788]: 426)

Likewise, he cautions that allowing judges to be impeached on the basis of inability, as opposed to misconduct, exposes them to a similar danger:

An attempt to fix the boundary between the regions of the ability and inability, would much often give scope to personal party attachments and enmities to advance the interests of justice or the public good. The result, except in the case of insanity, must for the most part be arbitrary ...

(1961 [1788]: 498)

Nevertheless, despite these dangers, the legislature's capacity to carry out impeachments was seen as a vital and necessary mechanism of the last resort for preventing the abuse of power. With respect to the executive, for instance, Jay invokes the specter of impeachment as the ultimate reason that presidents would refrain from making treaties that served their own private interests at the expense of the public good. He concludes *Federalist 64* by observing,

... we have reason to be persuaded that the treaties they make will be as advantageous as, all circumstances considered, could be made; and so far as the fear of punishment and disgrace can operate, that motive to good behavior is amply afforded by the article on the subject of impeachments.

(1961 [1788]: 425)

In a similar vein, Hamilton addresses those fearful of instantiating the judiciary with too much power by simply stating that the constitutional check provided by impeachment is sufficient for ensuring that the judiciary will not encroach on legislative authority. "This is alone a complete security," he succinctly writes (1961 [1788], 509).

In sum, the logic of constitution crafting that is so eloquently captured by the *Federalist Papers*, and which later spread out to the Americas and beyond, describes a world in which the threat of impeachment acts chiefly as a deterrent. Simply put, impeachment prevents tyranny ex ante, rather than punishes it ex post. It provides a clear motive for good behavior on the part of presidents and judges based on the desire to avoid a negative and costly outcome. Impeachment thus operates no differently from other general deterrence models, at least ideally.

To see this logic at work, consider the following stylized scenario captured in Figure 1.1. In this game there are two players, the executive and the legislature. The executive makes an initial decision about whether to engage in misconduct or not. Here, for the sake of simplicity we assume that what constitutes misconduct is clear to both players. The legislature then makes a subsequent decision about whether or not to impeach the executive. This leads to four possible outcomes, labeled as A to D. A obtains if presidents abuse their powers and the legislature impeaches them for doing so. B occurs if presidents abuse their powers and get away with it. C is defined by the president respecting the rule of law but getting punished by the legislature anyway, an infelicitous scenario that neatly captures the politicized outcome articulated by Hamilton above. Finally, D (deterrence) arises when presidents stay within the bounds of their power and keep their posts.

Assuming complete information (i.e., each player knows each other's preferences, each player knows that the other player knows his or her preferences, and so on), what is required for deterrence to work? In other words, what needs to be true about the players' preference ordering in order for D to be the unique subgame perfect equilibrium to this elementary game?

The answer is straightforward. First, presidents must prefer remaining in power to getting impeached (B > A; D > C). Given the various attempts

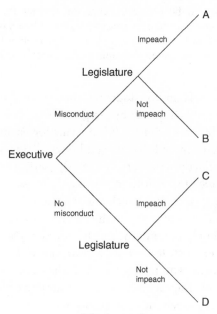

FIGURE I.I: The impeachment game.

made by Latin American presidents to overturn term limits and remain in office, this hardly seems an unreasonable assumption to make about executive preferences. That Latin American presidents also routinely face criminal prosecution or exile once they leave office (e.g., see Carey, 2009) only further underscores the plausibility of this assumption. Second, however, we must also assume that the legislature opts for impeachment only when the president has actually overstepped his or her bounds (A > B; D > C). As long as Congress punishes transgressions and only transgressions, and the president knows this and wishes to keep his or her post, then he or she will be compelled to respect the rule of law. As in other versions of the standard deterrence model, the core implication is that impeachment remains entirely in the shadows.

A similar logic of deterrence also drives the slightly more nuanced SOP games. Pioneered by rational choice scholars of American politics, the standard SOP approach employs a basic spatial model to show how one branch of government – the president, the courts, or the bureaucracy – can be compelled to modify its behavior to avoid sanctions at the hands of the branches of government. In one of the more familiar applications of this approach, scholars treat US Supreme Court justices as policy seekers who face having their decisions overturned by a joint effort between the

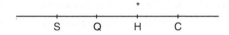

FIGURE 1.2: The separation of powers game.

House and the Senate (Gely and Spiller, 1990; Ferejohn and Weingast, 1992; Epstein and Knight, 1998; Harvey and Friedman, 2006). Assuming that the Court prefers to have its decisions stick, judges are thus forced to locate their decisions within the range (i.e., the win-set) that both legislative bodies find mutually acceptable.

Figure 1.2 depicts these three institutional actors on a single policy dimension running from left to right. For the US courts, this dimension is generally assumed to be the standard liberal-conservative dimension, where policies located on the far left correspond to the most liberal position and policies on the far right correspond to the most conservative position.[3] Assuming that actors try to maximize their preferences, that they know each other's preferences, and that preferences are single-peaked, the key to predicting judges' behavior lies in knowing the relative location of the various actors' preferences. In Figure 1.2, where Q is the status quo, and C, H, and S represent the ideal points for the Court, the House, and the Senate, respectively, the equilibrium of the game is again obvious. Because the Court is constrained to make decisions that fall within the win-set, or within the interval between H and S, the model tells us that the best the Court can do is set policy at H. Although the Court is able to move policy a bit closer to its ideal point, it is effectively constrained from setting policy anywhere it pleases.

Taken together, the virtue of the two models presented thus far lies in their simplicity and generality. They force us to be clear about the assumptions that are necessary for deterrence to work: complete information and a clear ordering of actors' preferences over outcomes. Yet the limitations of applying these standard theoretical models to contemporary Latin American politics are also immediate and obvious. Namely, these models consistently predict that the very sorts of crises that we have been describing cannot occur in equilibrium. Reality disagrees: actors who should adjust their behavior to avoid costly consequences somehow

---

[3] In some contexts, two dimensions may make more sense. For instance, in their recent analysis of the Mexican Supreme Court, Sánchez, Magaloni, and Magar (2011) reveal the importance of legal philosophy as a second salient dimension.

repeatedly fail to do so, leading to a world marked by gross inefficiencies and suboptimal outcomes. Inter-branch crises, like labor strikes, presidential vetoes, and wars, thus would seem to represent another version of the familiar Hicks paradox (cf. Cameron, 2000).

If traditional and modern SOP theories – theories that were, after all, born in the US context – wildly underpredict inter-branch strife, the standard comparative literature on Latin American presidentialism risks erring in the opposite direction. Starting with Juan Linz's seminal work on the perils of presidentialism, a prominent strain in the literature has long argued that presidentialist systems are inherently prone to conflict and institutional breakdown (Linz, 1990, 1994; Przeworski et al., 2000; Valenzuela, 2004, but also see Shugart and Carey, 1992; Mainwaring, 1993; Mainwaring and Shugart, 1997; Cheibub, 2007). In Linz's archetypal formulation, such systems suffer from a litany of intrinsic problems, ranging from the winner-take-all quality of elections to the ongoing dilemmas of dual legitimacy between the executive and legislative branches to the rigidities imposed by fixed terms.

Presidentialism, according to this view, is an institutional arrangement fraught with contradictions: the president is elected to represent the "whole people," but he or she is simultaneously a member of a particular political party. Likewise, a president is expected by his or her supporters to rule effectively, but is inevitably limited by the legislature, which also rightly claims to represent the people. Fixed terms compound these problems: presidents who manage to successfully navigate their jobs are forced to eventually leave office, whereas those who are miserable failures ostensibly have to remain for the duration. According to Linz and his followers, it was precisely for this last reason that presidential democracies throughout the mid-twentieth century tended to suffer from more regime breakdowns than did parliamentary systems. With no equivalent mechanism to the vote of confidence for getting rid of ineffective or highly unpopular presidents, militaries were that much more tempted to step in to end the associated gridlock and chaos that inevitably characterize such systems.

A decade on, Arturo Valenzuela (2004) astutely observed that even with the military now safely relegated to the barracks, elected governments throughout Latin America still remain vulnerable to many of the same vagaries and dysfunctional relationships outlined by Linz. Because of the enormous popular expectations placed on the office of the president, leaders often find their administrations blamed for any and all policy failures. Protests against specific policies therefore have a dangerous tendency to morph into the general demand of "Que se vayan todos!"

("Everyone must go!"). Moreover, despite the widespread belief that Latin American leaders are all-powerful, the vast majority of leaders lack sufficient legislative support to accomplish their objectives. Opposition parties have little incentive to cooperate with minority presidents, and even the support of members of president's own party cannot be guaranteed, particularly if the president's policies lose popular support. The result, as Valenzuela succinctly puts it, is that Latin American leaders are often forced to reign rather than rule (2004: 12).

Guillermo O'Donnell's (1994) highly influential notion of delegative democracy provides yet another take on the pathologies of presidentialist systems in Latin America. Starting with the basic observation that Latin American presidents govern as they see fit, O'Donnell chronicles the implications that this style of leadership carries for both vertical and horizontal accountability. Although checks and balances formally exist (i.e., the legislature and courts are imbued with various formal powers), presidents all but refuse to countenance them. Rather, claiming to be the nation's savior, presidents end up ruling by decree and through technocrats. Precisely because of this, however, they alone must bear sole responsibility for not only their successes, but also their failures. As a direct result, Latin American presidents thus find themselves vulnerable to a particular cycle of crisis in which the failure to adequately deal with economic or other sorts of political emergencies quickly moves them from a position of omnipotence to impotence.

Yet why so many Latin American politicians are seemingly unable to anticipate such cycles from playing out and adjust their behavior accordingly is rarely called into question. Notwithstanding the limits of human reasoning or the hubris of certain leaders, a fully coherent theory of institutional crisis requires explaining why, if sanctions are clearly in play, political actors open themselves to risk and often end up suffering the consequences. Rather than treat inter-branch crises either as an inevitable outcome of presidentialism writ large or as part of a broader syndrome of everything that is wrong with Latin American political culture, we need a framework that both helps account for this seeming paradox and explains why crises vary across administrations and institutions.

1.2 THE CORE ARGUMENT

My argument begins with the familiar premise that Latin American presidents enjoy two types of powers: de jure powers, such as the president's formal institutional powers specified by the Constitution, and de facto powers, such as the president's level of partisan support in Congress or their degree of public support (cf. Mainwaring and Shugart, 1997). Drawing on a series of off-the-shelf formal bargaining models due to Powell (1999), I then analyze (1) how the gap in the balance of these powers affects the likelihood of presidential crises, and (2) how expected shifts in that gap help trigger legislative and judicial crises. In so doing, I subsume several longstanding insights from the comparative literature on institutions, while at the same time explaining systematically why institutional instability varies across countries, time, and institutions.

1.2.1 Presidential Crises

To give a flavor of my theory of institutional instability and how it relates to conventional approaches, let me start with presidential crises. First, imagine a scenario in which the president enjoys a relatively high level of constitutional power, but lacks significant partisan powers. If the president has the proverbial last word in a given policy dispute, it is easy to conclude that he or she will be tempted to simply go it alone. Cox and Morgenstern (2002) describe just this sort of an equilibrium emerging in contexts where presidents face a recalcitrant Congress and have no other means at their disposal for enacting their legislative agendas (also see Jones, 1995).

Shift to a world in which legislatures can effectively sanction presidents who opt for this strategy, however, and the problem suddenly becomes more interesting. Under this latter scenario, the size of the gap between the president's partisan support and constitutional powers now not only affects the president's incentives to reign rather than rule, but also simultaneously increases the legislature's incentives to get rid of the rogue president. The trade-off comes down to this: on the one hand, the more formal policy-making powers the president concedes, the more likely it is that she will appease Congress and stave off a confrontation. On the other hand, the more powers she concedes, the more likely it is that she will end up unnecessarily limiting her own influence. Of course, if the president knows precisely how far she can push her powers before the legislature will balk, she will limit herself accordingly and the bargaining problem again disappears. But under the arguably more realistic assumption of incomplete information, the president is instead forced to take a calculated risk. And precisely because presidents are unable to perfectly gauge the point at which exerting their power triggers legislative sanctions, presidents who face this gap in powers sometimes push the envelope too far.

The claim that strong presidents with weak partisan support suffer from a particularly fatal combination of institutional traits, of course, is not new (Shugart and Carey, 1992; Mainwaring, 1993; Jones, 1995; Mainwaring and Shugart, 1997; Cheibub, 2002). Starting with Shugart and Carey's path-breaking work (1992), scholars have long recognized that not all presidents share the same degree of presidential powers, nor that all presidents are necessarily prone to the same level of crisis. Building on this observation, Mainwaring and Shugart concluded their seminal analysis of presidentialism in Latin America by speculating that

> Having weaker executive powers also means the cases in which presidents lack reliable majorities are less likely to be crisis-ridden, since the president has fewer tools with which to try to do an end run around the Congress.
>
> (1997: 436)

To date, however, the underlying logic of this interaction has not yet been fully explored, nor have subsequent empirical studies connected it systematically to the onset of presidential crises, let alone legislative or judicial crises. Rather, within the growing quantitative literature on early presidential exits, the debate has largely remained centered on whether mass protests and public scandals, divided government, and economic crises affect the likelihood that presidents will be forced from office early.[4] Indeed, very few of these studies even consider the role of formal presidential powers – let alone explore their interaction with partisan powers. The two exceptions of which I am aware, moreover, have uncovered little support for the view that presidential powers matter for this sort of crisis. Negretto (2006), for instance, finds that whether or not the executive enjoys decree or censure powers makes no difference in their early termination. Employing different

---

[4] Whereas most such analyses concur that presidents facing mass protests and/or scandals are especially vulnerable to being ousted (Hinojosa and Pérez-Liñán, 2003; Hochstetler, 2006; Pérez-Liñán, 2007; Kim and Bahry, 2008; Álvarez and Marsteintredet, 2009;), the evidence that the minority status of presidents and economic crisis affect presidential ousters is less clear cut. For instance, both Kim and Bahry (2008) and Álvarez and Marsteintredet (2009) find that presidential seat share in congress has a negative and significant impact on the likelihood of a presidential interruption. Along similar lines, Pérez-Liñán (2007) finds that presidents without a sufficiently large legislative shield are more likely to be impeached. In contrast, however, Hochstetler and Edwards (2009) find that seat share has no apparent effect. And Negretto (2006) finds that presidents are vulnerable only if the opposition is also ideologically arrayed against them. Meanwhile, only growth appears to be consistently negatively related to presidential ousters. Wealth has opposite effects in different models (cf. Álvarez and Marsteintredet, 2009; Hochstetler and Edwards, 2009), and inflation appears to have no systematic impact whatsoever (Kim and Bahry, 2008; Álvarez and Marsteintredet, 2009).

available formal measures of executive constraints, Kim and Bahry (2008) similarly conclude that such institutional arrangements have no effect. This book tells a different and more nuanced story. Specifically, I contend that both formal and partisan powers do matter for presidential crises, but that their effects are conditional on each other. In addition to the usual suspects such as mass protests and low popular presidential approval ratings, I argue that strong formal presidential powers do contribute to the onset of presidential crises, but only when the president is in the minority; likewise, minority presidents are vulnerable only when they already enjoy substantial formal presidential powers. Thus, expanding on the original intuition of Mainwaring and Shugart (1997), the bottom line is that contemporary presidential crises are fueled not by presidentialism per se, but by a certain mix of institutional and partisan features that precludes effective inter-branch bargaining.

1.2.2 Legislative and Judicial Crises

Having offered an alternative micro-level explanation of presidential removals, my theoretical framework also generates fresh insights into why presidents target the legislature and/or the courts. Shifting to a dynamic version of the theoretical model reveals that under certain conditions legislative and judicial crises are triggered by these branches' inability to commit to under-utilize their partisan powers to sanction presidents who overstep their bounds. As such, I argue that if presidents are able to anticipate such bargaining failures, then they can be tempted to preventively shut down recalcitrant legislatures and/or pack potentially hostile courts with their own supporters. Thus, in sharp contrast to the conventional view that presidents fancy themselves as somehow omnipotent and attack institutions to prove their prowess, the central implication that emerges is that it is precisely those presidents who anticipate being targeted themselves who are also the most likely to target other branches of power.

Consider for a moment leaders such as Fujimori, Chávez, or Correa. To be sure, such leaders have rightly earned labels of "populist," "authoritarian," or "caudillo." But aside from the fact that each of these presidents has taken steps to dismantle checks and balances, it is hard to ascertain whether such cultural or psychological traits sufficiently explain their behavior. Surely many Latin American leaders have had similar notions of grandeur. As Chapters 5 and 6 describe, however, what sets these leaders apart is that fact that each of them also clearly faced the specter of removal driven by the gap or expected gap in their presidential powers. In Fujimori's case, for instance, the president had already clashed with both the judiciary and the opposition-controlled legislature on multiple occasions. In the months leading up to the April coup, local newspapers repeatedly speculated about the president's ouster, and the possibility of impeaching Fujimori was openly discussed in Congress. As one keen observer of Peruvian politics writes, "By threatening to dismiss Fujimori, the legislature provided him with a strong motive to close Congress" (Kenney, 2004, 186). Following the coup in an interview with the Brazilian magazine *Veja*, Fujimori candidly admitted as much:

VEJA: Before 5 April, did you come to think that Congress would have deposed you, as it did in Brazil with Fernando Collor and with Andrés Peréz in Venezuela?

FUJIMORI: If I hadn't taken those measures, they would have deposed me. And not in order to moralize the country but rather to maintain their privileges.

(cited in Kenney, 2004, 207)

For leaders such as Chávez and Correa the threat of removal was perhaps more distant, but no less real. Both presidents came into office with extremely low partisan support and considerable leeway for unilateral action. In Venezuela, the outgoing opposition parties had moved to nonconcurrent elections ostensibly to reduce their losses. Although this institutional change effectively watered down Chávez's party's control over the legislature, he enjoyed tremendous popular support for his campaign promise to change the Constitution to bolster his own powers and rid the country of its corrupt elite. By using the constituent assembly to immediately take over both Congress and the courts, Chávez not only eliminated obstacles to getting his policies enacted, but also deprived the opposition of the major institutional routes it could have potentially used to get rid of him. As subsequent events like the botched coup attempt in 2002 or the failed recall referendum in 2004 suggest, Chávez's fears were well-founded.

Correa's exploits have a very similar flavor. In keeping with the book's central argument, Ecuadorian presidents are Latin America's most constitutionally powerful presidents, yet have also been the most vulnerable. In fact, in the decade leading up to Correa's election in 2006, no elected president had been able to complete his term in office. From the very beginning, Correa thus staked his presidency on creating a powerful constituent assembly that would allow him to overtake institutions controlled by the country's entrenched elite. Instead of running members of his party to serve in Congress, Correa campaigned on its wholesale reformation. Again, there is little doubt this had as much to do with securing his political life span as enacting his policy agenda.

As Ecuadorian expert Simón Pachano remarked at the time:

In this way, [the constituent assembly] that had been conceived as the basic tool for carrying out political reform was to become at the same time guarantor of the survival of his government.

(2007: 5)

The broader implication is that bargaining failures that stem from infelicitous institutional combinations not only prompt legislatures to seek to oust presidents, but also have the potential to provoke presidents to act preventively by launching attacks of their own. In this way, we begin to forge an understanding of both how particular types of crises emerge and how they potentially cascade across multiple institutions.

1.3 PLAN OF THE BOOK

The main goal of the book is to make sense of several substantively important puzzles about how SOP systems work – or fail to work. That the incidence and types of inter-branch crises vary significantly within Latin America makes it an especially compelling environment for investigating these questions. At the same time, given that Latin American countries are hardly the only ones afflicted by inter-branch crises – witness Yeltsin's self-coup in Russia; presidential impeachments in South Korea, the Philippines, and Madagascar; or the recent string of judicial attacks carried out in Pakistan – my analysis should provide valuable lessons for other struggling democracies around the world.

The remainder of the book is organized as follows. Chapter 2 introduces the Inter-Branch Crisis in Latin American (ICLA) dataset. Whereas the overarching concepts of political or institutional instability have long been fraught with confusion – "congenitally muddled," as Przeworski and company (2000) quip – here I attempt to clearly delimit inter-branch crises according to seven selection rules. Reassuringly, I find that the vast majority of the inter-branch crises that are captured using this protocol overlap with most of events that are commonly treated as institutional crises by both the existing quantitative and case study literatures. What is more, the succession criteria I develop further reveal that most of the cases included by my coding scheme tend to raise similar normative alarms; thus, we are not in any obvious danger of mixing a few actual crises with otherwise mostly legitimate instances of checks and balances or broader institutional reform. The second part of the chapter then turns to present an overview of the main empirical patterns and puzzles that drive the rest of the book. Disaggregating the data into three key types of inter-branch crises – presidential, legislative, and judicial – the rest of the chapter traces the extent to which each variant occurs over time and across countries, as well as which types of crises tend to cluster together and/or to repeat over time.

Chapter 3 presents the general theoretical framework that guides the rest of the book. Throughout, I draw extensively on formal models of crisis bargaining from the international relations literature, making particular use of Powell's 1999 theory of bargaining in the shadow of power. This approach supplies the micro-foundations for the familiar insight that presidents with strong formal powers and weak partisan support are particularly crisis prone, both in terms of generating presidential ousters but also, and perhaps less obviously, in spawning preventive presidential attacks on legislatures. All else equal, the theory underscores that it is the fundamental disparity between the president's de jure and de facto powers that provokes inter-branch crises, but that the core underlying mechanisms differ depending on the particular type of crisis. Asymmetric information prevents presidents at risk from easily appeasing their legislative opponents, whereas the legislature's inability to credibly commit to not exploit the president's potential loss of partisan powers drives the president to preventively attack Congress.

The next two chapters take the implications of the theory to the data. Chapter 4 exploits the quantitative data on legislative-executive relations contained in the ICLA dataset to evaluate the core hypothesis that the interaction of de facto and de jure presidential powers fuels presidential crises. Whereas the emerging literature on presidential crises tends to dismiss the role of formal presidential powers, here I deploy a battery of statistical tests to show that such conclusions are clearly premature. In line with my theory, concentrating substantial formal powers in the presidency does increase substantially the likelihood that presidents will be targeted by their legislative opponents, but only when the president is effectively already in the minority.

Chapter 5 adopts a mixed-methods approach to examine whether presidential attacks on legislatures are consistent with the dynamic version of the bargaining model. I begin by estimating a series of statistical models to evaluate the multiple testable implications associating legislative crises with the preventive strike logic. Specifically, I explore how well the theory's predictions regarding the combination of presidential powers, past experiences, relative costs, and timing hold up to empirical scrutiny. The second part of the chapter then analyzes four of the most high-profile cases of legislative crisis in contemporary Latin America: Peru in 1992, Guatemala in 1993, Venezuela in 1999, and Ecuador in 2007. The overarching goal in this section is to draw on a range of qualitative evidence (1) to assess whether these presidents had compelling reasons to believe that they were at risk of being removed and (2) to determine when, how, and why they came to view the elimination of Congress as key to their own survival.

Chapter 6 extends the bargaining framework to courts. In sharp contrast to the existing literature on judicial independence, I argue that judicial manipulation is triggered by presidents' drive to survive. Drawing on numerous examples, I show how the capacity of judges to alter the core parameters that determine the legislature's threshold for ousting the president transforms courts into especially valuable targets for presidents at risk. The chapter then returns to the ICLA dataset to examine systematically the testable implications of my argument, ruling multiple alternative hypotheses out along the way. Chapter 7 summarizes the main findings of the book and considers the implications for future research on institutional instability in emerging democracies.

2

Inter-Branch Crises in Latin America

This chapter has two main goals. The first is to clarify what the term "inter-branch crisis" means and to specify how it is measured. The second is to introduce the ICLA dataset and begin to explore some basic empirical patterns of institutional instability in Latin America. Along the way, the chapter presents seven selection rules that are used to determine which sorts of conflicts rise to the level of inter-branch crises and how such crises are counted. To evaluate the validity of these measurement rules, I consider whether the results tend to capture the various types of institutional crises that are commonly identified in the existing literature. As an additional check on whether the measures are conceptually sound, I also employ a "succession criterion," which ultimately casts doubt on the alternative possibility that checks and balances are functioning properly in the region. Applying these selection rules to eighteen Latin American countries between 1985 and 2008, the second half of the chapter then sketches the first general portrait of which types of inter-branch crises are more and less common, when and where they tend to occur, and the extent to which they cluster together.

2.1 DEFINING AND MEASURING INTER-BRANCH CRISES

When presidential systems function normally, political elites may fundamentally disagree over policy issues, but tend to resolve their differences through bargaining and compromise. When such systems fail, inter-branch bargaining breaks down and institutional crises reign. Perhaps nowhere has this tendency been more apparent than contemporary Latin

America, a region notorious for resolving its political problems by forcing presidents out of office early, dissolving legislatures, and sacking courts. Throughout the book, I define an inter-branch crisis as an episode in which one branch of government challenges the composition of another branch of government. Such crises can simply involve the survival in office of pivotal political actors (i.e., the president) or, more abstractly, may refer to changing the median voter in the court or the legislature.

To capture these sorts of high-stakes events systematically, I employ the following criteria:

- Selection Rule 1: Executives, Legislatures, and Courts
- Selection Rule 2: Presidents and Multimember Bodies
- Selection Rule 3: Institutional Composition Is at Stake
- Selection Rule 4: Initiation, Not Resolution
- Selection Rule 5: Number of Targets Equals the Number of Crises
- Selection Rule 6: Single versus Sequential Crises
- Selection Rule 7: Duration, Democracy, and Time in Power

The first three rules specify which actors and actions matter. Because I am ultimately interested in explaining the emergence of inter-branch crises, not their particular resolution, the fourth rule clarifies that inter-branch crises are determined by the institutional actors' threats and actions, not by any particular outcome. Thus, I include all attempts by one branch to remove another that fail as well as those that succeed. The fifth and sixth rules clarify how individual crises are counted. Although certainly other selection rules could reasonably be developed, here my goal is to devise and implement consistently a protocol that transforms what are often highly complex episodes into discrete observations. As such, the number of crises coded follows both the number of targeted branches and, in the case of multiple attempts, their timing, target, and nature. Finally, the seventh rule further delimits the types of administrations and the duration of the crisis. Let me start with the key actors.

2.1.1 Selection Rule 1: Executives, Legislatures, and Courts

I focus exclusively on institutional crises that involve at least two of the three major branches of the national government (the executive, the legislature, and/or the high court(s)). More specifically, I concentrate on four main aggressor–target combinations: (1) executive–legislative, (2) legislative–executive, (3) executive–judicial, (4) legislative–judicial. The various permutations that I consider range from simple, so-called dyadic crises that involve one branch trying to remove another to more complex institutional battles that draw in all three branches of government. As such, the definition comprises everything from the textbook presidential impeachments in Brazil (1992) and Venezuela (1993) to the self-coups carried out in Peru (1992) and attempted in Guatemala (1993) to the judicial-presidential debacle that swept Ecuador in 2004–2005. I then employ the terms "presidential crisis," "legislative crisis," and "judicial crisis" to denote distinct subtypes of inter-branch crises in terms of the particular branch that is targeted for removal.

In specifying the criteria used to identify inter-branch crises, it is also useful to be clear about the sorts of events that are excluded by virtue of the types of institutional actors involved. In terms of the target of the attack, I exclude all institutional conflicts in which one of the three main branches is not the object of the attack. President Cristina Kirchner's controversial decision to force the head of the Argentine Central Bank to resign in 2010 obviously constitutes a kind of institutional crisis, but is not an inter-branch crisis per se.

Turning to the aggressor branch, I employ the following exclusion rules: first, I do not treat the court as an independent aggressor.[1] Since Hamilton, scholars have rightly viewed the court as the least dangerous branch. Not only does the court lack both the purse and the sword, but it does not possess any means to initiate attacks against the other two branches.[2] Even in instances where the court appears to play an independent role, the ability to bring suits against the other branches always requires a third party (Ríos-Figueroa 2011). For example, in Ecuador in 2007 the Supreme Court asked Congress to strip President Correa's immunity for alleged defamation, but the charges were initially brought before the Court by a third party.[3] In Paraguay, the Supreme Court threatened President Cubas with impeachment for noncompliance in the Oviedo case, but Congress had asked the Court to review the case in the

---

[1] Note that in Helmke (2010) I allow the court to be an aggressor branch. Empirically, only six cases were coded as instances of court–legislature attacks, and in each of these cases the court did not initiate the suit. Moreover, on closer examination, some of these cases do not fit with Selection Rule 2 because they would not have changed sufficiently the composition of the legislature.

[2] As Hamilton puts it, "the judiciary is beyond comparison the weakest of the three departments of power ... it can never attack with success either of the other two; and ... all possible care is requisite to enable it to defend itself against their attacks" (*Federalist 78*).

[3] *Latin American Weekly Report* (*LAWR*), August 30, 2007.

first place (Pérez-Liñán, 2007: 31). In Guatemala, the CICIG and the Attorney General formally accused President Otto Pérez Molina of corruption, prompting the Supreme Court to permit that Congress decide whether to strip him of immunity.[4] Certainly, once a case is in the court, the justices' decisions can profoundly affect the institutional composition of either branch. Indeed, for this very reason, I shall argue that even though the court cannot unilaterally attack other branches, it is an especially attractive institution to control, and hence an important target for the other two branches.

Along the same lines, if Congress plays no role in a presidential crisis or vice versa, then I do not treat it as an inter-branch crisis per se. This effectively means that some of the presidential failures noted by other scholars are excluded from my analysis. For instance, Argentine President Raúl Alfonsín resigned several months early in the midst of a severe economic crisis, but without any clear pressure to do so from Congress. Bolivian President Carlos Mesa had to submit his resignation twice to Congress before it was accepted, but at no point did Congress threaten him with removal. Following the same logic, I include the dissolution of the Venezuelan and Ecuadorean Congresses by constituent assemblies, which were convened and controlled by Presidents Chávez and Correa, respectively, but exclude the dissolution of the Colombian Congress, which was called for by the multiparty constituent assembly in 1991, and not spear-headed by President Gaviria.[5]

Of course, the inter-branch element of any given political crisis may vary. As experts routinely note, some presidents are primarily targeted by Congress, whereas in other instances, the military or the "street" plays a much bigger role. Consider President Jamil Mahuad's overthrow by a military–civilian junta in 2000, which culminated with Congress' blatantly false declaration that the Ecuadorian president abandoned his post. Or think of Argentinean President Fernando de la Rúa's resignation in 2001, which came on the heels of demands by the Peronist opposition for his impeachment following mass protests. In both of these instances,

---

[4] *LAWR*, August 27, 2015.
[5] In response to a broad social movement demanding constitutional reform, President Barco issued a decree formally convoking a referendum in 1990, which was upheld by the Supreme Court. Elections for the constituent assembly took place subsequently under President Gaviria. Once elected, the members of the constituent assembly decided to dissolve the legislature. The president supported the process, but did not dominate it, and most of the old legislators were ultimately reelected (see Fox et al., n.d.)

Congress played a marginal but still identifiable role in these ousters. In subsequent chapters I therefore check the robustness of my empirical results by eliminating cases in which the inter-branch element of the crisis is present, but borderline.

2.1.2 Selection Rule 2: Presidents and Multimember Bodies

To be counted as an inter-branch crisis, attempts to alter the composition of the targeted branch must also reach a certain level and/or number of members. Specifically, with respect to the executive, I include efforts to remove only the president, not his or her ministers. Although countries such as Ecuador and Brazil suggest that the interpellations and dismissal of cabinet members may go hand in hand with an eventual threat to the president, by themselves such incidents do not necessarily alter control over the executive branch and, thus, consistent with the first selection rule, are not treated as inter-branch crises.

Identifying the thresholds for legislative and judicial crises is more complicated. There is obviously a difference that needs to be captured between Correa's forced removal of fifty-seven Ecuadorian legislators who refused to grant the constituent assembly plenipotentiary powers and a single Brazilian deputy being stripped of immunity so that he can face corruption charges. The former clearly suggests that the institution is being attacked, whereas the latter attack could simply indicate that an errant legislator is being held to account for his misdeeds.[6] To attempt to address this difference systematically, I include only those instances in which multiple members of courts and legislatures are targeted. The easiest cases that meet this threshold are those in which all members of the Congress or the courts are attacked, such as the self-coups launched by Fujimori and Serrano. Harder cases are ones in which fewer than the majority of members are targeted. Here I rely on the details of the case to determine whether the number of members attacked clearly undermines or fundamentally changes the functioning of a given institution.[7] For instance, in Bolivia in 1993, President Sánchez de Lozada's party initiated impeachment charges against two of the most senior members of the

---

[6] Of course, even removing one judge or legislator could change the median member. However, in the absence of information about ideal points for all judges and legislators in Latin America during this time period, I employ the criteria described above.

[7] Additional information about coding is available at http://www.gretchenhelmke.com/uploads/7/0/3/2/70329843/icla_codebook.pdf.

Supreme Court for corruption. Following their removal, the Court was hamstrung; the vacancies went unfilled and the Court could not select a new president. For these reasons, the case is included as an institutional crisis even though the entire bench was not removed (Rodríguez Veltzé, 2001).[8]

2.1.3 Selection Rule 3: Institutional Composition is at Stake

Building on my initial definition of an inter-branch crisis, the basic threshold condition that I employ involves at least one branch of government threatening to undermine the survival or change fundamentally the composition of another branch of government. Other sorts of threats or attacks that threaten to change an institution's powers but do not raise issues of composition are not included. Therefore, although attempts to strip a court's jurisdiction or expand or contract the executive's decree powers may occur alongside threats to replace or remake a key branch of government, I do not code them as inter-branch crises unless the composition of the targeted branch is also on the table.

Obviously, the particular types of threats or attacks will vary with the branch of government that is being targeted, as well as with the constitutional and statutory provisions in place for a given country at a given time. For presidents, the modes of early removal by Congress range from impeachment or forced resignation under the shadow of impeachment to the declaration of incapacity or abandonment of post to shortening the president's mandate. Nor do all threats require the same degree of effort or coordination among the opposition. In many cases, for instance, there is a higher bar for impeaching the president than for removing him or her on grounds of mental or moral incapacity.[9] The constitutional clause on mental incapacity contained in the

[8] *LAWR*, June 23 and July 7, 1994.

[9] Constitutional provisions for declaring a president physically or mentally incapacitated exist in nine Latin American countries (Chile 1980; Colombia 1886, 1991; Costa Rica 1949; Ecuador 1978, 1998; El Salvador 1983; Guatemala 1985; Nicaragua 1995, 2000; Peru 1979, 1993; Venezuela 1999). Only in El Salvador and Nicaragua (1995) is the threshold for removing the president due to incapacity (2/3) higher than it is for initiating the impeachment process (1/2). In the remaining seven countries, the threshold is either the same (Guatemala 2/3; Nicaragua (2000) 2/3; Peru 1/2; Venezuela 1/2) or lower (Colombia (1886, 1991)1/2; Costa Rica 1/2; and Ecuador (1978, 1998) 1/2). Note that the threshold in the lower house for removal due to incapacity is also lower in Chile (1/4), but then requires majority votes by the Court and the Senate in order to remove the president from office (see Kada, 2003; Pérez-Liñán, 2007).

Ecuadorian Constitution allowed the legislative opposition to move much more quickly and effectively against Abdalá Bucaram than it would have been able to had the opposition pursued a regular impeachment trial (Mejía Acosta and Polga-Hecimovich, 2010).

In turn, judges may be impeached or forced to resign from their posts as well, but the composition of high courts can also be manipulated by the other branches through stacking, dissolving, and/or dismantling the court. As Castagnola and Pérez-Liñán (2011) point out, in Bolivia the independence of the judiciary has been repeatedly crushed through a combination of these methods. Peru offers another familiar case in point. Five years after the complete overhaul of the judiciary in 1992, Fujimori's cronies in Congress impeached several justices on the Constitutional Tribunal for daring to rule against the president's bid for a third term in office. Rendered inquorate, the high court simply ceased to function.

By comparison, executives tend to have fewer means at their disposal to attempt to alter fundamentally the composition of the legislature (see Pérez- Liñán, 2007). Obviously, there is the extraconstitutional route of calling out the tanks, which succeeded for Fujimori but failed for Serrano. Yet despite some observers' worries, other Latin American leaders have generally not tried to follow this path. Instead, presidents such as De León (1993), Chávez (1999), and Correa (2007) have tended to work through popularly elected constituent assemblies to permanently dissolve and reconstitute the legislature. Others have only temporarily suspended the legislature, as both Chamorro (1992) and Ortega (2008) did in Nicaragua.

2.1.4 Selection Rule 4: Initiation, Not Resolution

To qualify as an inter-branch crisis, the attack may succeed in toppling the institutional actors targeted, but need not. All that is necessary is that an inter-branch conflict escalates to the point where one branch is threatening to remove the other.[10] Consistent with other scholars of presidential crises (Hochstetler, 2006; Pérez-Liñán, 2007; Marsteintredet and Berntzen, 2008; Hochstetler and Edwards, 2009), this rather broad

---

[10] For coding purposes, we used the following rule as a minimum threshold: actors in one branch had to publicly issue the threat. In other words, rumors or suspicions that an *autogolpe* or a presidential removal were afoot do not qualify. Likewise, we do not consider dares by one branch for the other to remove it. For instance, in 1999, in the midst of his call to revamp the legislature and the courts, Chávez dared the legislature to try to remove him from power (see Chapter 5).

criterion allows me to include such well-known cases as the failed attempt made by the Colombian Congress to impeach President Samper in 1995–1996 for allegedly accepting drug money during his electoral campaign, or the two separate unsuccessful attempts to get rid of Paraguayan president Gonzalez Macchi in 2001 and again in 2002. By including all such attempts at removal, we also pick up several other lesser known incidents, such as the foiled attempt to impeach former Ecuadorian president Durán-Ballén in 1995 following the ouster of his Vice President Alberto Dahik, or threats the same year by the congressional opposition to impeach Nicaraguan president Violeta Chamorro for refusing to promulgate the legislature's constitutional reforms.

Likewise, with respect to legislative and judicial crises, selecting cases based on initiation rather than resolution enables me to incorporate the most notorious examples – Fujimori's and Serrano's *autogolpes*, Menem's court-packing, Chávez's use of the constituent assembly to eliminate checks on his power, Morales' dismantling of the Bolivian judiciary – along with several additional lesser known cases, ranging from León Febres Cordero's unsuccessful attempt to pack the Ecuadorean Supreme Court following its unpopular decision in 1985 to release a banker charged with corruption associated with a major banking scandal to Andrés Pastrana's ill-fated attempt to dissolve the Colombian Congress through a referendum in 2000.[11]

2.1.5 Selection Rule 5: Number of Targets Equals the Number of Crises

In general, the number of branches targeted in a given conflict determines the number of inter-branch crises. In the event where one branch simply attacks another, the case is coded as a single inter-branch crisis.[12]

---

[11] To distinguish between executive attacks on the judiciary and legislative attacks on the judiciary, I consider whether it is the president's party launching the attack or not. In the former case, I treat this as an executive–court conflict; in the latter case, I treat it as a legislative–court conflict.

[12] Of course, it is important to recognize that some portion of these crises will indirectly involve a third branch of government. Consider presidential impeachments. Throughout Latin America, Congress is always required to initiate impeachment proceedings, but, depending on the constitutional provisions, they may be obligated to turn the trial of the president over to the judiciary. Or, take any one of the numerous instances in which the court is targeted by the executive branch. Although the precise rules vary, in each and every Latin American constitution presidents are at least formally precluded from removing or replacing judges unilaterally. Thus, even if the main conflict is between the president and the court, the legislature (or the legislative commission for

Conflicts, however, can sometimes generate multiple crises, a phenomenon that I come back to below. For instance, when one branch simultaneously targets two branches, two branches target one another, or one branch targets a second and the second branch targets a third, multiple types of crises occur. Because I ultimately estimate separate models for presidential, legislative, and judicial crises, I avoid the obvious problem of double- or triple-counting observations, while precluding the need to make arbitrary decisions about whether a given president cared more about controlling one branch more than another. Thus, I code Hugo Chávez's and Ramiro de León Carpio's decisions to remake the legislature and the courts as both legislative crises and judicial crises. In the *autogolpes* carried out by Fujimori and Serrano, the legislature also threatened to remove the executive, so these events created all three types of crises simultaneously.

2.1.6 Selection Rule 6: Single versus Sequential Crises

Another issue is whether to code multiple attempts by one institution to target another as one crisis or as separate crises. The basic rule I employ revolves around the timing and the distinctiveness of the attempt. A largely single sustained effort that spans multiple years (e.g., the Colombian Congress's attempts to remove President Samper on receiving drug money for his campaign in 1995–1996) is treated as a single crisis. Likewise, sustained attempts to remove multiple members of a given institution are also coded as a single inter-branch crisis. Kirchner's removal of individual Argentine justices sequentially offers a case in point; ultimately, the impeachment trials were spread out over a couple of years but involved a single strategy to get rid of Menem's justices one at a time.

Conversely, when one branch targets another twice under different charges in consecutive years I code each episode as a separate inter-branch crisis. Congress tried and failed to impeach Paraguayan President González Maachi first in 2001, and then tried and failed again under different auspices in 2002; thus, I code each attempt as a separate crisis.[13]

---

the constituent assembly) is necessarily pulled in. Menem's ploy to stack the Argentine Supreme Court in 1990 required the approval of the Peronist-dominated legislature, as did Duhalde's decision a decade later to rescind his attempt to impeach Menem's so-called automatic majority (Helmke, 2005).

[13] Note that because of the unit of analysis in the dataset, administration-ordered dyad-year, we cannot code more than one type of crisis per administration-year. So, in the case of President Gonzalez Macchi, the Congress actually made multiple attempts to get rid of

Similarly, Morales' tactics and targets against the Bolivian judiciary palpably shifted from one year to another. In 2006, the new administration pressured incumbent judges on both high courts to resign. In 2007, the president instead used his majority in the legislature to target the Bolivian Constitutional Tribunal specifically for its refusal to countenance Morales' attempts to replace the Supreme Court justices by decree. In 2008, the administration embarked on yet another wave of attacks against any remaining Supreme Court justices who had dared to rule against him.

2.1.7 Selection Rule 7: Duration, Democracy, and Time in Power

Because I am focused on explaining the origins of inter-branch crises, I begin coding each crisis from the point in time at which a threat is manifest as opposed to when the case is finally resolved. For instance, for the *autogolpe* in Peru, I use November 1991 as the official start date, which is when the specter of an inter-branch crisis first became public, as opposed to April 1992, when the president finally succeeded in shutting down Congress and the courts. Determining the end date depends, in part, on whether the attack succeeded or failed. For successful attacks, I simply use the date on which the institutional actor or actors were removed.[14] For failed attacks, I use either the last date the crisis was covered in the news or, if available, the date on which the crisis was actually resolved.[15]

In addition, I limit the dataset to all democratic and semi-democratic administrations that lasted longer than six months. By democratic and semi-democratic, I mean governments that come to power under regimes that are considered to meet the minimal threshold for competitive

---

Macchi in 2002 alone, but I treat this as a single crisis. Likewise, in Ecuador, the legislature made multiple attempts to get rid of President Lucio Gutierrez in 2004, but we code this as a single presidential crisis in 2004.

[14] The two exceptions to this occurred in Brazil and the Dominican Republic, in which presidential mandates were shortened far in advance of the president leaving office. In these cases, I use the date that the agreement to shorten the mandate was reached as opposed to coding the entire presidential term as a crisis.

[15] If the case is mentioned only once in the *Latin American Weekly Report*, I code the duration as one month. If the case is mentioned repeatedly but the duration is unclear, I code it as lasting approximately six months from the start date, choosing either June or December as the end month depending on which is closest given the start date. The ICLA Codebook is available online at http://www.gretchenhelmke.com/uploads/7/0/3/2/70329843/icla_codebook.pdf

elections or interim governments that replace such governments (Przeworski et al., 2000; Mainwaring and Pérez-Liñán, 2014).[16] Because several countries in the dataset transitioned from dictatorship to democracy after 1985 (Guatemala (1986), Paraguay (1989), Chile and Panama (1990), Mexico (2000)), administrations that were in place prior to that time are excluded. Likewise, to avoid double-counting presidential crises, I exclude from consideration all extremely short-lived administrations, such as the three caretaker governments that ruled Argentina for less than two weeks combined following de la Rúa's resignation (Llanos and Marsteintredet, 2010), or Ecuadorian Vice President Rosalia Arteaga's administration, which lasted only two days following Bucaram's ouster.

2.1.8 Summary

Taken together, the foregoing seven selection rules allow me to clearly classify what is (and is not) an inter-branch crisis. The first three rules specify that only conflicts in which at least one of the three main branches of the national government (the executive, the legislature, supreme and/or constitutional court(s)) seeks to jeopardize another branch's constitution count. The fourth rule highlights the fact that inter-branch crises include all instances in which one branch of government threatens to target another branch for removal, regardless of the outcome. The next two rules clarify how crises are delimited and differentiated. The last rule provides additional scope conditions regarding the duration of the crisis and the nature of the regime.

2.2 THE INTER-BRANCH CRISES IN LATIN AMERICA DATASET

To construct the ICLA dataset, I began by drawing on the *Latin American Weekly Reports* (multiple years), a news publication that offers weekly coverage of political events across the region. Using the seven selection rules described above, a team of research assistants from the University of Rochester and I read through every *Latin American Weekly Report* published between 1985 and 2008 to

---

[16] With respect to Przeworski et al.'s (2000) coding of democracies, the only substantive difference is that I exclude Brazilian President Joao Figueredo (1979–1985), who was appointed by the military regime, and include Fujimori's government post-1990, which was at least initially elected under democratic rules. My rationale is that I ultimately want to understand why inter-branch crises emerge under democratically elected governments, even if such crises ultimately mean that such governments become semi-authoritarian.

TABLE 2.1: *Breakdown of Inter-Branch Crises*

Type of Crisis	Total Number of Attacks	Mean	Observations	Average Duration in Months
All Crises	89	0.05	1896	5.4
Leg-Exec	36	0.08	474	4.9
Exec-Leg	9	0.02	474	5.4
Exec-Jud	33	0.07	474	6.3
Leg-Jud	11	0.02	474	4.0

systematically identify presidential crises, legislative crises, and judicial crises launched by either the president or the legislature.

To transform these qualitative accounts into quantitative data, I then grouped all articles related to each crisis and created individual case histories containing a variety of information, such as which administration was in power, the start date of the crisis, which branch initiated the conflict and which branch was targeted, the specific type of threat involved, and the outcome of the crisis. My coding for each crisis was then checked using a variety of other primary country-specific sources, including Spanish-language national newspapers, interviews with political actors and country experts, and numerous relevant secondary sources.

The ICLA dataset covers eighteen Latin American countries (Argentina, Bolivia, Brazil, Chile, Colombia, Costa Rica, the Dominican Republic, Ecuador, El Salvador, Guatemala, Honduras, Mexico, Nicaragua, Panama, Paraguay, Peru, Uruguay, and Venezuela) from 1985 to 2008. The total number of observations in the dataset is 1,896. The main unit of analysis is the ordered inter-branch dyad for each administration-year. Here, the ordered inter-branch dyad simply refers to the following four main aggressor–target combinations described above. Because my ultimate aim is to explain why crises emerge or not, the dataset also contains all "noncases" for each unit of analysis in which an inter-branch crisis did not occur.

Between 1985 and 2008, there were a total of eighty-nine crises for 474 administration-years, as shown in Table 2.1. Thus, institutional crises in Latin America occurred nearly 20 percent of the time. If we switch to use administration-year ordered dyad as our baseline, we see that the incidence drops due to the denominator and also varies substantially across the different types of crises. Presidential crises and judicial crises launched by the executive occur 8 percent and 7 percent of the time, respectively, whereas legislative crises and judicial crises launched by the legislature occur only 2 percent of the time. The average duration for each type of crisis ranges between four and six months, with legislative attacks on the courts lasting the shortest amount of time and presidential attacks on the court lasting the longest.

2.2.1 Validity and Succession Criteria

It is broadly reassuring that the vast majority of the crises targeting presidents that I pick up using the seven selection rules overlaps with those covered by the existing literature on presidential crises in Latin America. Despite differences in coding and time frames, nearly 75 percent of cases that I code as presidential crises are also cited in the secondary literature (see Table 2.2).

Nearly all of the presidential crises identified by Valenzuela (2004), Pérez-Liñán (2007), Kim and Bahry (2008), Llanos and Marsteintredet (2010), and Mustapic (2010) are contained in the ICLA dataset.[17] Likewise, with the single exception of Paraguay 1994,[18] I include all of the cases between 1985 and 2005 that are listed by Hochstetler (2006) as either challenges to the president launched by the legislature or jointly by the legislature and the "street." I also include three additional cases that are classified by Hochstetler as involving only the street: Ecuador (1999), Argentina (2001), and Bolivia (2003). As mentioned above, protests arguably played the most important role in these presidential

---

[17] Note that the two major exceptions are Haiti and Argentina. First, because I limit my focus to Spanish- and Portuguese-speaking countries, I do not include Haiti in the dataset (cf. Valenzuela, 2004). The only other meaningful difference between my cases and the cases covered in the extant literature involves how the interim Argentine presidents post-2001 are treated. For instance, both Pérez-Liñán (2007) and Mustapic (2010) list Rodríguez Saá but not the other two short-lived presidents; by Rule 7, all such short-lived administrations are excluded from my dataset. Finally, Mustapic also includes both Alfonsín and Duhalde (2002–2003) as examples of ousted presidents, but because Congress was not involved in their resignations, by Rule 1 I do not treat these as inter-branch crises.

[18] Under my selection rules, there was no inter-branch crisis in Paraguay in 1994. To be sure, there were protests by peasants over agricultural reforms, as well as calls for General Oviedo to step down from the armed forces. Also, at certain points the government pact with the opposition in Congress broke down, but there were no concrete threats or actions taken to remove the president. The only potentially qualifying incident was an investigation into President Wasmosy's election as president of the Colorados, but there is no evidence that the investigation called for his removal or was followed up in a way that threatened his tenure (see *LAWR*, June 16 and 30, December 1 and 29, 1994).

TABLE 2.2: *Presidential Crises Validity Check*

Administration	Country	Crisis Onset	Sources
Siles Zuazo	Bolivia	1985	*Latin American Weekly Report*; Valenzuela (2004); Pérez-Liñán (2007); Kim and Bahry (2008); Edwards and Hochstetler (2009); Buitrago (2010); Mustapic (2010);
Sarney	Brazil	1987	*Latin American Weekly Report*; Mainwaring (1997)
Febres Cordero	Ecuador	1987	*Latin American Weekly Report*; Hochstetler (2006); Pérez-Liñán (2007); Edwards and Hochstetler (2009)
Borja	Ecuador	1990	Pérez-Liñán (2007); Mustapic (2010)
Paz Zamora	Bolivia	1991	Pérez-Liñán (2007)
Borja	Ecuador	1992	*Latin American Weekly Report*; Mustapic (2010)
Fujimori	Peru	1991	Valenzuela (2004); Hochstetler (2006); Pérez-Liñán (2007); Marsteintredet and Berntzun (2008)
Collor	Brazil	1992	Valenzuela (2004); Hochstetler (2006); Pérez-Liñán (2007); Kim and Bahry (2008); Marsteintredet and Berntzun (2008); Mustapic (2010)
Pérez	Venezuela	1992	Valenzuela (2004); Hochstetler (2006); Edwards and Hochstetler (2009); Mustapic (2010)
Serrano	Guatemala	1993	Valenzuela (2004); Pérez-Liñán (2007); Kim and Bahry (2008); Marsteintredet and Berntzun (2008); Edwards and Hochstetler (2009); Mustapic (2010)
Balaguer	Dominican Republic	1994	Valenzuela (2004); Pérez-Liñán (2007); Kim and Bahry (2008); Mustapic (2010)
Durán-Ballén	Ecuador	1995	*Latin American Weekly Report*
Chamorro	Nicaragua	1995	*Latin American Weekly Report*
Samper	Colombia	1995	Hochstetler (2006); Pérez-Liñán (2007); Marsteintredet and Berntzun (2008); Edwards and Hochstetler (2009)

Wasmosy	Paraguay	1996	*Latin American Weekly Report*; Hochstetler (2006); Marsteintredet and Berntzun (2008)
Alemán	Nicaragua	1997	*Latin American Weekly Report*
Bucaram	Ecuador	1997	Valenzuela (2004); Hochstetler (2006); Pérez-Liñán (2007); Kim and Bahry (2008); Marsteintredet and Berntzun (2008); Edwards and Hochstetler (2009); Mustapic (2010)
Cubas	Paraguay	1998	Valenzuela (2004); Hochstetler (2006); Pérez-Liñán (2007); Kim and Bahry (2008); Marsteintredet and Berntzun (2008); Edwards and Hochstetler (2009); Mustapic (2010)
Cardoso	Brazil	1999	Latin American Weekly Report
Mahuad	Ecuador	1999	Valenzuela (2004); Hochstetler (2006); Pérez-Liñán (2007); Kim and Bahry (2008); Marsteintredet and Berntzun (2008); Edwards and Hochstetler (2009); Mustapic (2010)
Pastrana	Colombia	2000	Latin American Weekly Report
Fujimori	Peru	2000	Valenzuela (2004); Hochstetler (2006); Pérez-Liñán (2007); Marsteintredet and Berntzun (2008); Edwards and Hochstetler (2009)
De la Rúa	Argentina	2001	Valenzuela (2004); Hochstetler (2006); Pérez-Liñán (2007); Kim and Bahry (2008); Marsteintredet and Berntzun (2008); Edwards and Hochstetler (2009); Mustapic (2010)
González Maachi	Paraguay	2001	Pérez-Liñán (2007)
González Maachi	Paraguay	2002	Marsteintredet and Berntzen (2008); Pérez-Liñán (2007)
Chávez	Venezuela	2002	Hochstetler (2006); Edwards and Hochstetler (2009)
Sánchez de Lozada	Bolivia	2003	Valenzuela (2004); Hochstetler (2006); Pérez-Liñán (2007); Kim and Bahry (2008); Marsteintredet and Berntzun (2008); Edwards and Hochstetler (2009); Mustapic (2010)
Bolaños	Nicaragua	2004	Pérez-Liñán (2007)

(continued)

TABLE 2.2: (*continued*)

Administration	Country	Crisis Onset	Sources
Bolaños	Nicaragua	2005	*Latin American Weekly Report*; Edwards and Hochstetler (2009)
Duarte	Paraguay	2005	*Latin American Weekly Report*
Gutiérrez	Ecuador	2004	Acosta and Polga-Hecimovich (2010); Marsteintredet and Berntzun (2008); Edwards and Hochstetler (2009); Mustapic (2010)
Gutiérrez	Ecuador	2005	Acosta and Polga Hecimovich (2010); Marsteintredet and Berntzun (2008); Edwards and Hochstetler (2009); Mustapic (2010)
Lula	Brazil	2005	*Latin American Weekly Report*
Palacio	Ecuador	2005	*Latin American Weekly Report*
Correa	Ecuador	2007	*Latin American Weekly Report*
Ortega	Nicaragua	2007	*Latin American Weekly Report*

34

ousters, but in each of these cases the legislature also mattered. In Ecuador, there were calls within Congress to impeach Mahuad in March 1999.[19] In Argentina, the legislature's calls for impeachment were arguably the last straw in getting de la Rúa to step down early (Pérez-Liñán, 2007: 180). Following the violence associated with the protests in Bolivia, Congress played a similar role in getting Sánchez de Lozada to abandon his post.[20] The rest of the cases included in my dataset stem either from threats or failed attempts to remove presidents, which had not been previously uncovered by the literature, or from my inclusion of more recent cases.

Unfortunately, there is no comparable literature on legislative or judicial crises in Latin America with which to directly compare my data.[21] That said, with respect to legislative attacks, it is obviously a good sign that my coding rules cover the most egregious well-known cases (i.e., Fujimori in 1991–1992 and Serrano in 1993). Moreover, the fact that I ultimately identify relatively few legislative crises with my coding protocol fits well with the general sense that Latin American legislatures are now the least endangered branch (Pérez-Liñán, 2003, 2007). Likewise, my coding rules retrieve all of the most notorious examples of judicial manipulation, ranging from Menem's court-packing scheme to Morales' recent attempts to dismantle the Bolivian judiciary, as well as incorporate systematically the various failed efforts by Latin American presidents and/ or legislatures to remake the courts.[22]

In addition to passing these basic sorts of external validity checks, however, we also want to make sure that the coding rules are generally picking up cases that reflect the overarching normative conception of such inter-branch disputes as crises. The problem comes down to this: how can we tell the difference between the sorts of institutional failures or breakdowns that we want to capture and, for want of a better phrase, sincere

---

[19] *LAWR*, March 16, 1999.   [20] *LAWR*, February 25, 2003.

[21] A new historical dataset on judicial tenure for 18 Latin American Countries between 1904 and 2010 is the most closely related, but these data do not distinguish between manipulation, as I define it, and routine changes to the composition of the court (Pérez-Liñán and Castagnola 2014).

[22] Once the data on judicial crises were complied, I checked my coding with the following country experts: Catalina Smulovitz (Argentina); Aníbal Pérez-Liñán and Andrea Castagnola (Bolivia and Paraguay); Lisa Hilbink, Druscilla Scribner, Javier Couso (Chile); Juan Carlos Raga (Colombia); Dan Brinks, Diana Kapiszewski, Matthew Ingram, Matthew Taylor (Brazil); Julio Ríos-Figueroa, Beatriz Magaloni, Arianna Sanchez, Eric Magar (Mexico); Pilar Domingo, Rachel Seider, Borja Díaz Rivillas, Sebastián Linares, Elena Martínez Barahona (El Salvador, Honduras, Nicaragua, Guatemala).

attempts to improve or reform existing institutions? After all, if presidents or judges commit crimes and are impeached for them, isn't this rather a sure sign that checks and balances are working well? If constitutions aren't functioning properly, shouldn't popularly elected presidents be allowed to demand their reform?

Unfortunately, considering whether or not the formal rules for removal are followed takes us only so far. Fujimori clearly took extraconstitutional measures to dissolve the legislature and courts, but most contemporary institutional crises in Latin America have occurred well within the letter, if not the spirit, of the law. Taking at face value what the actors involved in the crisis claim they are doing is arguably even more problematic. Menem, after all, insisted that he was adding justices to the Argentine Court merely in order to handle increased demand by litigants – never mind that doubling the size of the court tended to slow down the decision-making process. Chávez, Correa, and Morales famously, and often all too convincingly, have invoked the "will of people" to justify their wholesale elimination of existing institutional checks and balances. Even Fujimori came up with a litany of reasons for why his *autogolpe* was in the nation's best interest.

Where means and words potentially mislead, focusing on the process of succession can better help us to discern institutional crises from normal checks and balances. Obviously, no institutional changes or reforms are ever entirely neutral (Przeworski, 1991; Knight, 1992; Boix, 1999), yet when one branch not only alters the composition of another, but also dominates its succession, then this is a probably a good indication that something is awry. Although we obviously do not have information on what would have happened in the cases where attempts were made and failed, for those that succeeded the pattern is clear enough.

Consider presidential crises (see Table 2.3). As in the United States, when Latin American presidents are removed from power early it is generally expected that vice presidents will take their place (Mustapic, 2010). But in the thirteen instances across Latin America where legislators have pushed presidents out of power early, in only four cases (Brazil in 1992, Bolivia in 2003, Ecuador in 2000 and 2005) have they actually been replaced by their vice presidents. In nearly every other case, the person who was chosen as the successor was not even from the same political party or faction as the ousted president.[23]

---

[23] Since 2008, succession following presidential ousters has also been partisan. In 2009, the Honduran president, Manuel Zelaya, and his vice president went into exile. Zelaya was

TABLE 2.3: *Presidential Succession (1985–2008)*

President/Party	Replaced by VP	Successor/Party Affiliation
De la Rúa/UCR	No	Duhalde/PJ
Siles Zuazo/MNR	No	Paz Estensorro/MNR
Sánchez de Lozada/MNR	Yes	Mesa/Independent
Collor/PRN	Yes	Franco/PRN
Bucaram/PRE	No	Alarcón/ARF
Mahuad/DP	Yes	Noboa/DP
Gutiérrez/PSP	Yes	Palacio/Independent
Serrano/MAS	No	De León Carpio/Independent
Cubas/Colorado	No	González Macchi/Colorado
Balaguer/SCR	No	Fernández/DLP
Pérez/AD	No	Velásquez/Independent
Sarney/PMDP	No	Collor/PRN
Fujimori/Peru 2000	No	Paniagua/AP

To be sure, in some instances there simply was no vice president waiting in the wings to take the helm. Between 1858 and 1999, for instance, the Venezuelan Constitution had no provision for a vice president. When Carlos Andrés Pérez was suspended in 1993, therefore, the head of Congress temporarily took power until Congress could designate a successor. In Argentina, Carlos "Chacho" Álvarez had already resigned from Argentina's first coalition government over a bribery scandal a little more than a year before de la Rúa was forced from power. In the space of few weeks Congress designated no fewer than four interim presidents; each was from the Peronist opposition. And in Paraguay, where President Cubas was impeached for allegedly having had his own Vice President Luis Argaña assassinated, Congress stepped in to designate someone from the rival Colorado faction.

In other instances Congress simply refused outright to countenance incumbent vice presidents. Not surprisingly, for instance, in Guatemala, Serrano's vice president was quickly deemed unacceptable in the wake of the failed self-coup. In Ecuador, the president of Congress engineered Vice

replaced by Roberto Micheletti, who was president of the National Congress. Although both Zelaya and Micheletti were Liberals, they were political rivals and Zelaya later changed his party. In 2012, the Paraguayan president, Fernando Lugo, was impeached and replaced by his vice president, who was from a different party. In 2015, the Guatemalan president, Otto Pérez Molina, resigned amid corruption allegations and was replaced by his vice president, who was from a different political party. Finally, in 2016, the Brazilian president, Dilma Rousseff, was suspended and replaced by her vice president, Michel Temer, who was also from a different political party.

President Rosalia Arteaga's ouster and took over the post himself. And when Fujimori fled to Japan in 2000 there was no question but that Congress would skip over his vice president and appoint a caretaker president from the opposition. Where presidents' mandates were instead shortened by Congress – Bolivia in 1985, Brazil in 1990, the Dominican Republic in 1996 – an opposition candidate won and took power directly.

Likewise, among the handful of legislative crises included in the dataset, employing the succession criterion reveals that presidents not only managed to alter fundamentally the composition of legislatures, but they and their parties immediately reaped the benefits. Fujimori's Cambio '90 had only 17.8 percent of the seats in the lower house of Congress before the self-coup, but comfortably controlled the majority thereafter. Under Chávez, the MVR won only around 25 percent of the legislative seats in the 1999 elections, but utterly dominated the new Congress, at least up until 2010. Meanwhile, in Ecuador Correa began his term without a single seat in Congress, but his party took over the constituent assembly and then effectively controlled the plurality in Congress.

Turning to the judiciary, a similar story emerges. Menem may have claimed that he was increasing the number of judges on the Supreme Court to alleviate case backlog, but he chose his tennis partner, his law firm partner, and various party hacks to fill the posts (Verbitsky, 1993; Larkins, 1998). In Ecuador, Gutiérrez twice packed the Ecuadorian Supreme Court with judges solely on the basis of whether or not they were acceptable to his ever-shifting coalition partners (Basabe and Polga-Hecimovich, 2013). In Venezuela, Chávez took a page out of Fujimori's playbook and kept the judiciary under provisional status, enabling him to easily remove and replace judges who dared to disagree with him (Brewer-Carías, 2010). Meanwhile, in Bolivia Morales skirted the opposition by unilaterally replacing judges on the Supreme Court by decree and leaving the Constitutional Tribunal inquorate. To be sure, in a handful of cases, such as Eduardo Frei's push to increase the number of justices on the Chilean Supreme Court in 1997, the degree of partisan control is much less obvious. But, in the great bulk of the judicial crises contained in the dataset, the way in which succession has been handled helps lays bare the lie of mere reform.

2.2.2 Patterns of Institutional Instability

Taken together, these data provide the first comprehensive view of institutional instability in contemporary Latin America across all three branches of government. Figure 2.1 traces out the trajectories for each

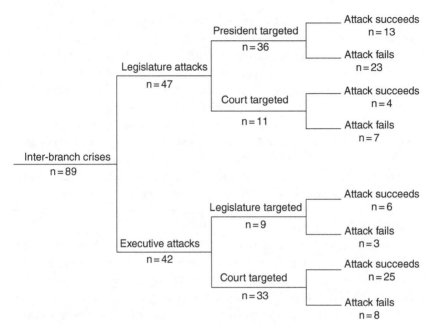

FIGURE 2.1: Patterns of inter-branch crises.

type of inter-branch crisis culminating with their success or failure. Raw counts of the number of crises that fall under each node or outcome are also given. Starting from the left-hand side of the figure and moving toward the right-hand side, the first main branching point distinguishes instances in which the legislative branch instigates the attack (upper branch) from instances in which the executive branch does so (lower branch). The second set of branching points differentiates among the respective targets. Legislatures attack either executives or courts; executives attack either legislatures or courts. The four possible sets of outcomes include:

1. Legislative attacks on presidents that either succeed in removing the president from office early or fail to do so
2. Legislative attacks on courts that either succeed in restructuring the composition of the court or not.
3. Executive attacks on legislatures that restructure the composition, dissolve, or suspend the legislature or fail to do so
4. Executive attacks on courts that either succeed in restructuring the composition of the court or not.

It is especially interesting to consider the distribution of crises in light of the increasingly common contention coming out of the literature on contemporary presidential crises in Latin America that legislatures, long considered weak and ineffective, are exhibiting a kind of newfound supremacy (Carey, 2005; Pérez-Linan, 2005, 2007; Marsteintredet and Berntzen, 2008). Figure 2.1 instead reveals that legislatures overall are only slightly more aggressive than executives. Compared with the executive branch, the legislative branch initiated 53 percent of all inter-branch crises (47 of 89). Of course, the distribution of targets between the two aggressor branches is quite different. Whereas legislative attacks on the president outpace legislative attacks on the court by about four to one, presidential attacks on the court outstrip presidential attacks on the legislature by three to one.

Moreover, even though only six legislatures were closed compared with the thirteen executives who have been successfully ousted, the success rates for the executive outstrips the legislative branch by roughly two to one. Whatever legislative supremacy exists thus appears to be generated mostly by the executive's initial reluctance to target the legislature, and not by what happens once such an attack occurs.[24]

Factoring in judicial crises further challenges standard claims of legislative dominance. Although legislative action is always necessary for taking legal action against the court, in the vast majority of judicial crises the executive is behind the attack. What is more, executive-backed assaults on the judiciary are generally much more successful than opposition legislative attacks on the courts. Presidents succeed in getting the legislature to remake courts more than 75 percent of the time, whereas opposition legislatures alone succeed in doing so only 36 percent of the time.

Turning to temporal trends, the data confirm O'Donnell's skepticism that Latin America's democracies would consolidate over time (1999: 175–194). With the exception of the late 1980s, in which institutional

---

[24] Whereas the main focus of this book rests on understanding the onset of different types of inter-branch crises, note that scholars have made considerable headway recently in addressing the related question of which types of presidential challenges succeed or fail in removing leaders from office. For instance, both Hochstetler (2006) and Pérez-Liñán (2007) highlight the importance of mass protests in removing challenged presidents from office. Hochstetler and Edwards (2009) further refine this by estimating a Heckman selection model that distinguishes presidential challenges from failures. They find that both the deaths that occurred during a mass protest and the president's partisan status help predict whether a president survives a challenge or not. To date, however, I am not aware of any similar studies that distinguish failure and success for legislative or judicial crises; thus, both constitute obvious areas for further research.

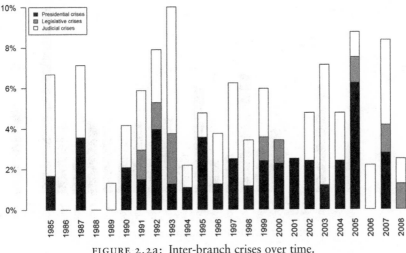

FIGURE 2.2a: Inter-branch crises over time.

attacks occurred at an average rate of 3 percent for all administration-year ordered dyads, the overall rate of crises has been rather consistent over time. Considering the data in five-year increments, the overall percentage of crises jumped to around 6 percent between 1990 and 1994, and then stayed at around 5 percent between 1995 and 2008 (see Figure 2.2a). Switching the denominator to the legislature–executive ordered dyad, presidential crises nearly doubled from 4 percent (three attacks out of 81 administration-years) during the last five years of the 1980s, to 8 percent (eight attacks out of 103 administration-years) during the early 1990s, and then leveled off at around 9 percent (25 attacks out of 290 administration-years) between the late 1990s and 2008 (see Figure 2.2b). Similarly, judicial crises have occurred with roughly the same degree of regularity throughout the period, varying at a rate between 4 percent during the late 1980s and then between 4 and 6 percent for each five-year increment thereafter (see Figure 2.2d). The picture for legislative crises, which are rarer, is different. There are three temporal clusterings: the first around the early 1990s (3.1%), the second at the turn of the century (1%), and the third between 2005 and 2008 (3.7%), with a new crop of political outsiders turning to popularly elected constituent assemblies in order to dissolve their legislatures (see Figure 2.2c).

If most institutional crises have been spread out relatively evenly over the last three decades, cross-sectional comparisons reveal far more systematic variation. Although few countries in the region have entirely

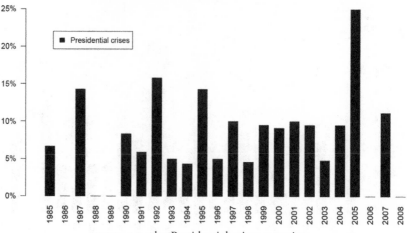

FIGURE 2.2b: Presidential crises over time.

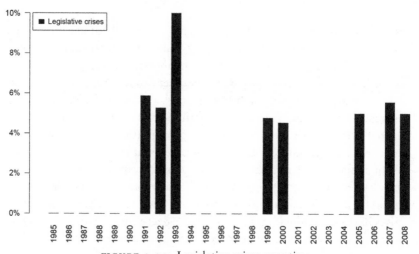

FIGURE 2.2c: Legislative crises over time.

escaped institutional instability, Figure 2.3 demonstrates that the distribution of inter-branch crises across the region has been quite uneven. Using the administration-year ordered dyad again as the baseline, Ecuador stands out as a kind of regional basket case with institutional crises occurring nearly 18 percent of the time (21 crises out of 120 observations) (see Figure 2.3). Crises have occurred between 5 and 10

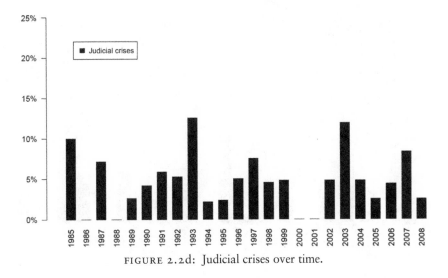

FIGURE 2.2d: Judicial crises over time.

percent of the time in Argentina, Bolivia, Chile, Guatemala, Nicaragua, Paraguay, Peru, and Venezuela. By contrast, Brazil, Colombia, the Dominican Republic, Honduras, and Uruguay have had crises less than 5 percent of the time, whereas Costa Rica, El Salvador, Mexico, and Panama have had none at all.

The overall picture of inter-branch strife thus generally mirrors the scholarly consensus about variation in the quality of democracy across the region (Hagopian and Mainwaring, 2005). Of course, given that the more egregious instances of institutional instability are often factored into such rankings, it would be surprising only if quality was not at least loosely associated with crises.

Interestingly, Figure 2.3 also shows that among the most institutionally unstable countries, there are repeated bouts of the same types of crises (i.e., multiple presidential crises or multiple judicial crises), as well as rather consistent pairings of different types of crises within countries. The two most typical types of crises, presidential and judicial, have tended to go hand in hand in countries such as Argentina, Bolivia, Ecuador, Guatemala, Nicaragua, Peru, Paraguay, and Venezuela. In fact, only in Colombia, Brazil, and the Dominican Republic do we see presidents being threatened without the occurrence of a judicial crisis.[25]

---

[25] See Rodríguez-Raga (2011) for a description of the sorts of threats that have been waged by presidents against courts in Colombia.

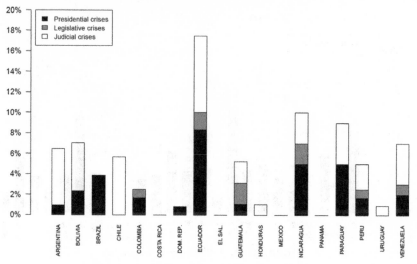

FIGURE 2.3: Inter-branch crises by country.

By contrast, Chile is the only country in which the executive has launched an attack on the judiciary without being attacked in turn.[26] Although there are plenty of countries in which legislatures go after presidents without themselves being targeted, in no country do we find presidents threatening legislatures without a reciprocal threat having been made or carried out.

To explore further how different types of crises cluster, I collapse the data to the administration level. Table 2.4 shows the various combinations of crises that occur within administrations. Remarkably, just 30 percent of all crises occur in isolation. Of these, only 15 percent (14 of 89) are confined to the "new institutional instability" discussed in the literature in which legislatures exclusively target presidents. Single crises in which executives target courts are almost as common (10 of 89). The vast majority of crises, however, were not one-off affairs. Most administrations that experienced one type of a crisis experienced at least another type as well. For example, in fully nine administrations in which a presidential crisis occurred, the executive also attacked the court. In other instances, we find reciprocal attacks between the legislature and the

---

[26] Note that in Honduras and Uruguay, judicial crises occurred without presidential crises, but they were initiated by the legislature, not the president.

TABLE 2.4: *Distribution of Crises within Administrations*

Type and Combination	Total Number of Crises	Administration[a]
Single Crises		
Presidential Crisis	14	Alemán, Balaguer, Cardoso, Collor, Cubas, de la Rúa, Fujimori (3), Lula, Mahuad, Samper, Sarney, Siles, González Macchi (2)
Judicial Crisis (E)[b]	10	Alarcón, Alfonsín, Duhalde, Kirchner, Paz Estenssoro, Aylwin (2), Morales (3)
Judicial Crisis (L)[b]	3	Córdova, Menem, Sanguinetti
Double Crises		
Presidential Crisis; Judicial Crisis (E)	22	Bucaram (2), Durán-Ballén (2), Febres Cordero (2), Paz Zamora (2), Pérez (2), Sánchez de Lozada (2), Wasmosy (2), Chávez2 (3), Guitiérrez (5)
Presidential Crisis; Legislative Crisis	6	Ortega (2), Palacio (2), Pastrana (2)
Judicial Crisis (L); Judicial Crisis (E)	7	Fujimori (2), Menem (2), Frei (3)
Judicial Crisis (L); Presidential Crisis	3	Borja (3)
Legislative Crisis; Judicial Crisis (E)	4	De León (2), Chávez (2)
Triple Crises		
Judicial Crisis (E); Judicial Crisis (L); Presidential Crisis	8	Bolaños (4), Duarte (4)
Presidential Crisis; Legislative Crisis; Judicial Crisis (E)	9	Correa (3), Fujimori 1st term (3), Serrano (3)
Presidential Crisis; Legislative Crisis; Judicial Crisis (L)	3	Chamorro (3)

[a] Numbers in parentheses refer to the number of crises under an administration.
[b] E refers to attacks on the judiciary by the executive branch and L refers to attacks on the judiciary by the legislative branch.

executive (Ortega, Palacio, Pastrana), two against one attacks against the court (Fujimori 2nd term, Menem, Frei), or cases involving pure aggression against the other two branches by either the president (De León, Chávez) or the legislature (Borja). Some administrations were even more crisis ridden. For example, under Bolaños and Duarte, the legislature targeted the executive, and both elected branches targeted the court. Under Correa, Fujimori, and Serrano, the legislature targeted the executive, while the president went after both the legislature and the court. And under Chamorro, the executive targeted the legislature, while the legislature launched attacks against both the president and the court. Clearly, presidents aren't the only ones who suffer from institutional instability.

2.3 SUMMARY

Inter-branch crises, to put it mildly, are not ordinary political conflicts. While institutional battles that lead political actors in one branch of government to sanction political actors in another could indicate that checks and balances are working rather well, there are reasons for skepticism. After all, the vast majority of experts in the region have tended to take precisely the opposite view, at least when presidents act as the main aggressors. What is more, although the formal rules often permit such actions – albeit by their letter, if not their spirit – we have found fairly consistent evidence showing that when the aggressor branch succeeds in changing its target's composition, the partisan balance dramatically tilts in the aggressor's favor. This is not to say that the courts or legislatures that were supplanted were perfect, nor that presidents who were removed from office early never engaged in corruption or malfeasance. But the process of succession that tends to occur in contemporary Latin America suggests that something other than simple redress or reform is often the driving force. If vice presidents rarely replace ousted presidents, the opposition loses majority control in a reconstituted legislature, and judicial posts are consistently manipulated for maximal political gain, then it is surely a stretch to conclude that institutions are working properly. Rather, as the next chapter shall go on to elaborate, the fundamental problem is that if checks and balances are generally intended to deter "bad" behavior, then the very fact that sanctions are being deployed at all is itself deeply puzzling.

Turning to the empirical data on inter-branch crises, several patterns emerge. First, inter-branch crises in Latin America occur with some degree of regularity. Unfortunately, there are no identical data for other parts of the world, so whether or not Latin America is particularly prone to this type of institutional instability we cannot say. We do know, however, that compared with other important political phenomena, the incidence of institutional instability in the region has been relatively high. Compared with the Third Wave democratic transitions in the region, which occurred in about 12 percent of all regime-years, inter-branch crises have broken out in a little less than 20 percent of all administration-years.[27]

Second, most of the variation in the data is cross-sectional, not temporal. Consistent with critics of democratic consolidation in the region, there has been no downward trend in the incidence of inter-branch crisis over the last three decades. If anything, the rate of crises has increased. The evidence for systematic cross-sectional variation, however, is compelling. The data clearly show that the so-called perils of presidentialism do not plague all Latin American countries equally. Rather, there appears to be a kind of bimodal distribution whereby roughly half of the countries in the region are relatively crisis free, whereas the other half suffers repeated bouts of institutional instability.

Third, there is also considerable variation across the three branches of government in terms of which branches launch attacks and which branches get targeted. In keeping with the formal rules surrounding removal, in most countries presidents and judiciaries are targeted far more frequently than legislators. Yet despite the fact that legislatures tend to have more institutional tools at their disposal for attacking other institutions, the overall aggression rates for executives and legislatures are roughly similar.

Finally, we have learned that many institutional crises do not occur in isolation. Although much of the recent literature on the new institutional instability in Latin America has focused exclusively on presidential crises spearheaded by the legislature, the data show that such crises are more frequently than not correlated with other types of institutional instability. The next chapter provides a unified theoretical framework inspired by the formal literature on crisis bargaining to make sense of these empirical patterns; subsequent chapters then return to the data to evaluate the theory's multiple testable implications against various alternative explanations.

---

[27] Note that throughout the book we use administration-year ordered dyads, which increases the denominator and, thus, drives down the frequency of inter-branch crises. However, for the purposes of this comparison, it makes sense to focus on administration-years. According to Mainwaring and Pérez-Liñán (2005: 20), transitions to democracy or semi-democracy within Latin America between 1978 and 1999 occurred 11.9 percent of the time.

Appendix

Inter-Branch Crises

Country	Administration	Year	Conflict Type
Argentina	Alfonsín	1987	Exec-Court
Argentina	Menem	1989	Exec-Court
Argentina	Menem	1993	Leg-Court
Argentina	Menem	1998	Leg-Court
Argentina	De la Rúa	2001	Leg-Exec
Argentina	Duhalde	2002	Exec-Court
Argentina	Kirchner	2003	Exec-Court
Bolivia	Siles	1985	Leg-Exec
Bolivia	Paz Estenssoro	1987	Exec-Court
Bolivia	Paz Zamora	1990	Exec-Court
Bolivia	Paz Zamora	1990	Leg-Exec
Bolivia	Sánchez de Lozada	1993	Exec-Court
Bolivia	Sánchez de Lozada	2003	Leg-Exec
Bolivia	Morales	2006	Exec-Court
Bolivia	Morales	2007	Exec-Court
Bolivia	Morales	2008	Exec-Court
Brazil	Sarney	1987	Leg-Exec
Brazil	Collor	1992	Leg-Exec
Brazil	Cardoso	1999	Leg-Exec
Brazil	Lula	2005	Leg-Exec
Chile	Aylwin	1991	Exec-Court
Chile	Aylwin	1992	Exec-Court
Chile	Frei	1996	Leg-Court
Chile	Frei	1997	Exec-Court
Chile	Frei	1999	Exec-Court
Colombia	Samper	1995	Leg-Exec
Colombia	Pastrana	2000	Exec-Leg
Colombia	Pastrana	2000	Leg-Exec
Dominican Republic	Balaguer	1994	Leg-Exec
Ecuador	Febres Cordero	1985	Exec-Court
Ecuador	Febres Cordero	1987	Leg-Exec
Ecuador	Borja	1990	Leg-Court
Ecuador	Borja	1990	Leg-Exec
Ecuador	Borja	1992	Leg-Exec
Ecuador	Durán-Ballén	1994	Exec-Court
Ecuador	Durán-Ballén	1995	Leg-Exec

Country	Administration	Year	Conflict Type
Ecuador	Bucaram	1996	Exec-Court
Ecuador	Alarcón	1997	Exec-Court
Ecuador	Bucaram	1997	Leg-Exec
Ecuador	Mahuad	1999	Leg-Exec
Ecuador	Gutiérrez	2003	Exec-Court
Ecuador	Gutiérrez	2004	Exec-Court
Ecuador	Gutiérrez	2004	Leg-Exec
Ecuador	Gutiérrez	2005	Exec-Court
Ecuador	Palacio	2005	Exec-Leg
Ecuador	Gutiérrez	2005	Leg-Exec
Ecuador	Palacio	2005	Leg-Exec
Ecuador	Correa	2007	Exec-Court
Ecuador	Correa	2007	Exec-Leg
Ecuador	Correa	2007	Leg-Exec
Guatemala	De León	1993	Exec-Court
Guatemala	Serrano	1993	Exec-Court
Guatemala	De León	1993	Exec-Leg
Guatemala	Serrano	1993	Exec-Leg
Guatemala	Serrano	1993	Leg-Exec
Honduras	Suazo Córdova	1985	Leg-Court
Nicaragua	Chamorro	1992	Exec-Leg
Nicaragua	Chamorro	1995	Leg-Court
Nicaragua	Chamorro	1995	Leg-Exec
Nicaragua	Alemán	1997	Leg-Exec
Nicaragua	Bolaños	2003	Leg-Court
Nicaragua	Bolaños	2004	Exec-Court
Nicaragua	Bolaños	2004	Leg-Exec
Nicaragua	Bolaños	2005	Leg-Exec
Nicaragua	Ortega	2007	Leg-Exec
Nicaragua	Ortega	2008	Exec-Leg
Paraguay	Wasmosy	1993	Exec-Court
Paraguay	Wasmosy	1996	Leg-Exec
Paraguay	Cubas	1998	Leg-Exec
Paraguay	González Macchi	2001	Leg-Exec
Paraguay	González Macchi	2002	Leg-Exec
Paraguay	Duarte	2003	Exec-Court
Paraguay	Duarte	2005	Leg-Exec
Paraguay	Duarte	2006	Leg-Court
Paraguay	Duarte	2007	Leg-Court
Peru	Fujimori	1991	Exec-Court
Peru	Fujimori	1991	Exec-Leg
Peru	Fujimori	1991	Leg-Exec

(*continued*)

(*continued*)

Country	Administration	Year	Conflict Type
Peru	Fujimori	1997	Exec-Court
Peru	Fujimori	1998	Leg-Court
Peru	Fujimori	2000	Leg-Exec
Uruguay	Sanguinetti	1985	Leg-Court
Venezuela	Pérez	1992	Exec-Court
Venezuela	Pérez	1992	Leg-Exec
Venezuela	Chávez	1999	Exec-Court
Venezuela	Chávez	1999	Exec-Leg
Venezuela	Chávez	2002	Exec-Court
Venezuela	Chávez	2002	Leg-Exec
Venezuela	Chávez	2003	Exec-Court

3

Institutional Crises as Bargaining Failures

Institutional crises generally elicit one of two responses. If the targeted branch has clearly violated the rule of law and the formal rules delivering punishments have been faithfully followed, then scholars may simply conclude that checks and balances are operating as they should. If neither of these conditions has been met, however, then observers tend to surmise that institutions are failing miserably. But, as we have glimpsed in the previous two chapters, conventional interpretations do not go far enough analytically. Whether or not institutional clashes are viewed as crises or necessary checks, the very fact that institutional relations have reached this stage is still fundamentally puzzling. For ideally, as Chapter 1 pointed out, either checks and balances should deter bad behavior ex ante or, if punishments serve instead as partisan tools, then targeted actors should adjust their behavior accordingly to avoid opportunistic sanctions. Why, then, might institutional actors fail to do so? Why, in short, do institutional crises occur at all?

The answer that this chapter develops draws on a series of strategic models inspired by the formal bargaining literature on war.[1] Using war as a theoretical analogue for institutional crises makes sense for a number of reasons. First, similar to inter-state relationships, there is no higher power enforcing institutional bargains; constitutions must be self-enforcing

---

[1] Schelling (1960) was the first to draw explicitly on the tools of game theory to study the onset of war. Since then, numerous other scholars have sought to refine and extend this approach to both inter-state and civil wars (see Bueno De Mesquita and Lalman, 1994; Fearon, 1995, 1998, 2004; Powell, 1999, 2002, 2006; Wagner, 2000; Slantchev, 2003; Smith and Stam, 2004; Fey and Ramsay, 2006, 2011).

(North and Weingast, 1989; Przeworski, 1991; Weingast, 1997; North, Wallis, and Weingast, 2009). Whether or not conflict or cooperation occurs in either domain largely depends on the incentives that institutional actors face. Second, as in the international arena (cf. Schelling, 1960), there is considerable evidence that actors from each branch of government weigh carefully the costs and benefits of available strategies before attacking actors in another branch of government. Fujimori debated over many months whether to attack the legislature and courts unilaterally by staging a self-coup, and decided to do so only once the prospect of his own removal at the hands of Congress grew and public support for these two institutions shrank (Kenney, 2004). Likewise, President Correa's plan to dissolve the Ecuadorian Congress rather than allow any members of his party to run for office was clearly rooted in the calculation that he would not have initially obtained anything close to a majority and thus would have been vulnerable to the same problems that plagued his predecessors (Conaghan, 2008). Anticipating how other actors will respond and adjusting one's behavior accordingly is the very essence of strategic behavior. Third, similar to the relationships between unitary states in the international environment, I shall argue that in presidentialist systems the relationship among presidents, legislatures, and judiciaries raises a host of familiar strategic problems rooted in asymmetric information and the inability to make credible commitments (cf. Fearon, 1995; Powell, 1999). Building on the familiar observation that Latin American presidents often find it difficult to underutilize their formal powers (Mainwaring and Shugart, 1997; Cox and Morgenstern, 2002), this chapter analyzes the combination of conditions under which legislatures face incentives to oust presidents, and presidents attempt to ameliorate that risk by launching a preventive strike against the legislature.

To be sure, the analogy between inter-state wars and institutional crises is not perfect. Branches do not seek territory from one another. The costs of battle in a dispute between legislators and presidents are less tangible, and (usually) less bloody, than in a full-scale war.[2] And although purely dyadic disputes certainly exist between two branches of government, as we shall see in Chapter 6, institutional crises that involve courts

[2] That said, several institutional crises have led to the exile or prosecution of leaders such as, Alemán, Bucaram, Collor, Cubas, Fujimori, Pérez, Sánchez de Lozada, and Serrano. What is more, some crises have also resulted in the deaths of protesters. For instance, twenty-five were killed in Argentina in the mobilizations against the government in 2001; forty-six were reported killed in Venezuela in the attempted coup against Chávez, while in Bolivia in 2003 there were approximately 100 deaths reported (Hochstetler, 2006: 412).

are often triadic in nature. Yet the wager here is that these important substantive differences do not prevent us from drawing on the general theoretical tools developed in this literature to illuminate the dynamics of institutional relations in Latin America. As with any applied modeling enterprise, we learn both from seeing how much of the empirical puzzle we are able to get right with these tools and from discovering how much remains to be understood.

The rest of the chapter proceeds as follows. As a first cut, I begin by drawing on the familiar crisis bargaining subgame popularized in the early formal literature in international relations to show the simplest scenario under which institutional crises across all three branches can emerge. The comparative statics that this basic model generates allow us to connect the costs and benefits each branch faces to a set of clear predictions about the onset and evolution of institutional crises. Following a brief discussion of the limits of this preliminary modeling effort, the second half of the chapter turns to analyze a more nuanced bargaining scenario between the president and the legislature.

Adopting Powell's (1999) theory of bargaining in the shadow of power, I reexamine the familiar relationship between the president's de facto and de jure powers. Contrary to several recent empirical studies of presidential crises, I demonstrate that it is the disparity between these two types of powers that puts presidents at risk. Specifically, I show that the more the president's formal powers outpace her partisan powers, the more incentives legislative opponents have to oust such presidents. Under complete information, a president may well be able to stave off such attacks by offering legislatures a deal. But under the arguably more realistic assumption that presidents lack information about precisely how much they need to concede, the gap opens up the possibility that presidents will miscalculate and overshoot the limits of their power. Moving to a dynamic version of the model, I then turn to examine informally the conditions that lead presidents at risk to stage preventive attacks on legislatures. Taken together, this theoretical framework not only provides an intuitively appealing explanation for how each particular type of inter-branch crisis emerges, but also reveals how these two types of institutional crises are fundamentally connected to one another.

3.1 A BASIC MODEL OF INSTITUTIONAL CRISES

To start to understand why institutional crises emerge, I begin by drawing on the classic crisis subgame common to the early formal theory literature

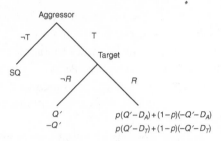

FIGURE 3.1: Inter-branch crisis game.

in international relations (e.g., Bueno De Mesquita and Lalman, 1994; Fearon, 1995; also see Signorino, 1999; Signorino and Yilmaz, 2003).[3] Assuming complete and perfect information in a single-shot game, the model casts interbranch crises en toto as the result of a basic cost–benefit calculus.

Figure 3.1 contains two players, which I generically refer to as the Aggressor branch and the Target branch. Each makes a single decision. At the first node, the Aggressor decides whether or not to threaten the Target with an attack against the Target's survival (T, ¬T). If the Aggressor does not issue a threat to attack, the game ends with the status quo (SQ) upheld. Alternatively, the Target is forced to choose between resisting (R) and not resisting (¬R), where the latter results in a revision of the status quo, Q', in favor of the Aggressor. If the Target instead chooses to resist, the outcome is Fight.

Following standard practice, the status quo payoffs are normalized to (0, 0). If a threat is waged and the Target acquiesces, then the Aggressor and Target each receive $(Q', -Q')$ respectively, where Q' denotes the stakes of the political conflict and $Q' > 0$. As an example, a president who successfully rewrites the constitution gains Q' by increasing her control over policymaking. Conversely, legislators under the new constitutional regime lose $-Q'$, which can be associated with the new distribution of policymaking power. In the event that the Target resists, fighting ensues. At this node, the payoffs are determined by a lottery, p, representing the probability that the Aggressor will win, the stakes involved in the crisis, Q', and the costs that the Aggressor and Target branches pay for engaging in an institutional crisis, D_A and D_T, respectively.

---

[3] A version of this section appeared in Helmke (2010).

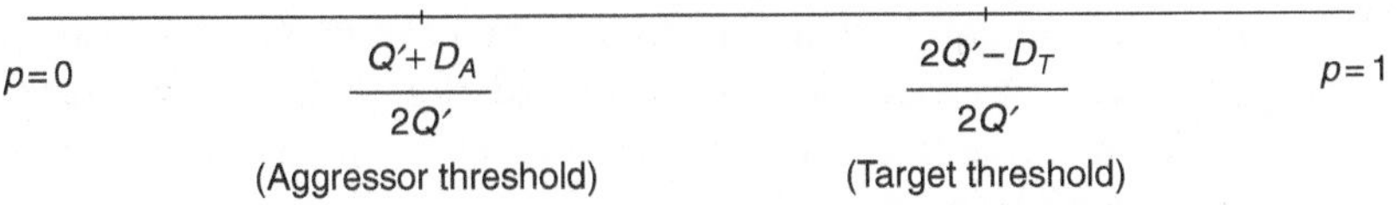

$p=0$	$\dfrac{Q'+D_A}{2Q'}$	$\dfrac{2Q'-D_T}{2Q'}$	$p=1$
	(Aggressor threshold)	(Target threshold)	

FIGURE 3.2: Comparative statics from inter-branch subgame.

Assuming that each branch knows its own payoffs and that each branch knows the other branch knows its payoffs and so forth, the solution to the game is straightforward. Here, the central intuitions hinge on each player's threshold for fighting. Working backward, the Target's threshold for fighting is $p < (2Q' - D_T)/2Q'$. Accordingly, the Target will resist as long as the probability that the Aggressor will lose is sufficiently high relative to D_T and Q'. Increasing the stakes effectively lowers the Target's threshold for fighting (i.e., the Target will challenge at greater levels of p). Increasing the costs, D_T, has the opposite effect. Note that for the Target's threshold to obtain, that is $0 < p < 1$, the costs must always be equal to or lower than the value of stakes ($D_T \leq 2Q'$). In the special case where fighting is costless, $D_T = 0$, Targets always prefer to resist, as long as $Q' > 0$.

In turn, the Aggressor's threshold to attack is $p > (Q'+D_A)/2Q'$. Provided that the Aggressor's expectations of success fall above this threshold, she will always prefer to threaten rather than stick with the status quo. Like the Target, increasing the stakes and lowering the costs lower the Aggressor's threshold for fighting (i.e., she will attack at lower levels of p). For the Aggressor's threshold to obtain, the key assumption is that $Q' > D_A$. Intuitively, if the stakes are not sufficiently high relative to the costs, then the Aggressor will not deviate from the status quo.

Figure 3.2 summarizes the thresholds for each actor in terms of the parameter p. As such, the strategy profile in which the Aggressor is deterred from threatening the Target [¬T, R] is supported whenever p falls to the left of the Aggressor's threshold. The strategy profile in which the Aggressor threatens and the Target does not resist [T, ¬R] is supported whenever p falls to the right of the Target's threshold. The strategy profile in which fighting occurs [T, R] is supported whenever p falls in between the two players' thresholds. How large the parameter space is for fighting compared with the other two outcomes depends on the values the players attach to Q' and D_A and D_T. Assuming $D_A = D_T$, higher stakes increase the space in which fighting occurs; higher costs shrink it. Taken together, we now have a baseline model that tells us how institutional crises can occur in equilibrium. Given that we have previously lacked a systematic account with clear micro-foundations, this is surely an advance. At the same time, however, the model is also clearly limited in several important respects.

First, as shown in Helmke (2010), empirical support for the standard crisis subgame model, which estimates crises across all three branches of government simultaneously, is mixed. On the one hand, there is considerable evidence that the model works, more or less, as expected for predicting the Aggressor branch's behavior. The probability of launching an attack against another branch increases in stakes and probability of success, and decreases in legitimacy costs.[4] On the other hand, the model struggles to explain the Target's response. Although stakes apparently continue to matter, neither expectations of losing nor legitimacy costs seem to affect the Target's decision to acquiesce or fight back.

One possible explanation for this discrepancy takes us back to the comparative statics provided by the preliminary model. Recall that the Target's threshold $p < (2Q' - D_T) / 2Q'$ means that the decision to resist hinges on the value of D_T. Where $D_T = 0$, Targets will always choose to fight as long as $p < 1$. However, if it is the case that Aggressors with lower levels of legitimacy are themselves more likely to initiate crises, then the parameter space for fighting increases, just not in the particular way we have modeled. And as suggested in Helmke (2010), perhaps the reason that we do not uncover the effects of legitimacy on the Target's response is precisely because of the Aggressor's initial decision to select themselves into crises.

At the same time, the current model fails to allow for the possibility that the Target's prior actions matter. Put differently, at this stage of the modeling dialogue, we have allowed only for the Aggressor branch to behave strategically. Although the Target eventually maximizes its choice, only the Aggressor acts in anticipation of that choice. Because of this, we still therefore have not yet fully answered the question in our original puzzle of why both branches act in seemingly suboptimal ways.

---

[4] The key parameters estimated in the model (2010) were operationalized as follows: to capture Q and Q', I drew on existing measures of formal institutional powers from Alemán and Tsebelis's (2005) scale for executive and legislative powers and Ríos-Figueroa (2011) for judicial powers. As a proxy for the legitimacy costs of waging institutional attacks against a given branch of government, I used public opinion data contained in the Latinobarómetro (1995–2008) for each branch of government. Finally, to capture p, I drew on information contained in the ICLA dataset that records the number of crises that each targeted branch has been involved in previously and the outcome of those crises.

To remedy this requires moving to a more flexible model that allows us to capture not just the strategic choice of one player but the strategic interactions between both players.

Another plausible objection to this preliminary modeling effort is that the assumption of complete information is most certainly unrealistic. Although perhaps this assumption is not as strong as it appears in the international relations literature, domestic political actors often do not share the same interpretation of the likelihood of prevailing in a crisis. Nor will political actors necessarily grasp perfectly the costs that the other is willing to tolerate by initiating or exacerbating an institutional crisis. Interim Argentine President Eduardo Duhalde was certainly caught off guard when his attempts to get rid of the Supreme Court were met by the justices handing down decisions that pushed the country to the brink of economic collapse (see Helmke, 2005). As a result, it makes sense to turn to a theoretical framework that allows us to incorporate asymmetric information into the bargaining game.

Finally, a fundamental problem with the subgame model involves its pliability, at least in the following sense. By depicting institutional crises in such generic terms (i.e., Aggressors and Targets as opposed to, say, presidents and legislatures) we impose a kind of substitutability among the three branches that obscures some important differences. After all, as other scholars have cogently argued, the offensive advantage always lies, at least constitutionally, with the legislative branch (Pérez-Liñán, 2007). Of course, presidents do have sanctioning tools at their disposal, but they are often much harder to use. Courts, in turn, do not unilaterally initiate crises, but often get caught in the fray. As such, we need a theory that allows us to explore, first and foremost, the conditions under which the legislature faces incentives to use its sanctioning powers against the president and then connect these to the onset of other types of institutional crises. In short, we need an analytical framework that is more closely connected to how real world institutional crises unfold across institutions and over time.

3.2 EXECUTIVE-LEGISLATIVE BARGAINING UNDER THE THREAT OF REMOVAL

To address these various concerns, the following sections informally extend Powell's (1999) game theoretic model of inter-state bargaining in the shadow of power to explain the onset of presidential and legislative crises. Building on this discussion, Chapter 6 will take up separately the emergence of judicial crises. Here, the logic of bargaining – and, more interesting for our purposes, bargaining failures – revolves around the following three components. First, we need to again specify who the actors are and what they are bargaining over. As we have seen, in the literature in international relations the standard setup is that states bargain with each other over how to divide territory. In this context, the focus is on how the legislative and executive branches grapple with the president's power to set policy. As such, I assume that presidents with strong legislative powers effectively control more of the policymaking "pie" relative to the legislature than presidents who lack such powers.

At first glance, the assumption that presidents seek to maximize their formal policymaking powers and the legislative opposition seeks to minimize them may seem to clash with the observation that weak parties prefer to delegate power to the president (cf. Mainwaring and Shugart 1997). However, Negretto (2014) has shown that the apparent affinity between weak parties and strong presidents is driven by the fact that the president's party tends to be the most influential partner in reform coalitions, and not by the universal desire among opposition parties to overcome collective action problems.[5] The zero-sum setup adopted here thus dovetails with the recent literature on comparative institutions. It also allows us to build directly into our theoretical framework Madison's famous supposition that the central motivating force for each branch in a SOP system is to encroach on the powers of the others. Taken together, this setup enables us to explicitly link the intuition that strong presidential powers fuel institutional conflict with a micro-level account of why, when, and where such crises emerge.

The second element of my approach is to assume that bargaining occurs under the shadow of power, to borrow Powell's (1999) evocative phrase. Whereas in the international relations literature power is essentially conceptualized as the ability of one side to triumph over another on the battlefield, here power is treated simply as the capacity of the legislature to remove the president from office. This allows us to explicitly bring into play the partisan elements driving presidential crises, such as the minority status of the president. The third component of the framework incorporates the observation that political actors are often uncertain both

---

[5] Negretto's finding that opposition parties are generally reluctant to create strong executives also fits with the other longstanding claim that the powers of the executive increase as the influence of the executive on the constitutional process increases (cf. Mainwaring and Shugart 1997).

about the costs of the political crisis and, more fundamentally, about each other's tolerance for such costs. In most scenarios, politicians simply do not know whether the public will rally around presidents or desert them, or how exactly the international community will react. For instance, President Zelaya's ouster from Honduras in June 2009 brought strong international condemnation from an unlikely coalition of states, including the United States and Venezuela, as well as the suspension of much-needed financial aid. Meanwhile, public opinion was relatively evenly split along partisan lines. Conversely, the ouster of President Gutiérrez in Ecuador just a few years earlier received very little international attention and faced relatively little domestic opposition. At the other extreme, the recent resignation of Guatemalan President Pérez Molina has been celebrated as a sign that accountability is finally taking root. The key point here, though, is that even if politicians do know roughly how much they are willing to tolerate to achieve their ends, they may still be uncertain about the threshold for actors occupying the other branches. As we shall see in Chapter 5, Jorge Serrano's fundamental miscalculation during his self-coup provides a textbook example of asymmetric information. In short, political actors may know their own sensitivity to the costs associated with an institutional crisis, but not each other's.

Combining these three sets of observations into a single theoretical framework, the intuitively appealing story that emerges below allows us to connect the familiar gap between constitutional and partisan presidential powers not only with the presidents' incentive to rely more extensively on their constitutional powers (cf. Shugart and Carey, 1992; Cox and Morgenstern, 2002; Fish, 2009), but also with the legislative opposition's incentive to get rid of presidents who do so. Whereas under a scenario of complete information, presidents might still potentially commit to a bargain that would satisfy the legislature and thereby stave off impeachment, we discover that under asymmetric information, bargains, pace Powell (1999), are that much harder to strike. As a result, presidents push the limits of their power not merely because they lack congressional support, but because they are taking a calculated risk about whether or not they will be punished. Let me elaborate on how the president's dilemma emerges.

3.3 THE PRESIDENT'S DILEMMA

From Hugo Chávez in Venezuela to Daniel Ortega in Nicaragua to Cristina Fernández de Kirchner in Argentina, Latin American leaders are famous for operating at the limits of their power. This phenomenon, of course, is hardly confined to contemporary presidents. Between 1958 and 1991 Colombia was under a state of siege roughly 75 percent of the time (Archer and Shugart, 1997: 126). During this period presidents had enormous leeway to exercise broad emergency powers, powers that eventually spilled over into convoking a constitutional assembly and effectively closing the sitting legislature. Or take Brazil just after its most recent transition to democracy. Following the disintegration of his economic stabilization plan in the mid-1980s, Plano Cruzado, Brazilian President Jose Sarney repeatedly relied on his decree powers (Power, 1989: 204). His successor, Fernando Collor de Mello, continued this trend, virtually ruling by decree (Power, 1989: 207). Meanwhile, in Argentina, both Raúl Alfonsín and Carlos Menem increasingly invoked the line-item veto in order to protect their legislative prerogatives against the legislative opposition and, in Menem's case, even against his own party (Negretto 2014: 144). Carlos Menem, of course, also became infamous for his reliance on decrees of necessity and urgency (*decretos de necesidad y urgencia*), which allowed him to essentially dictate policy in the areas of taxation, salaries, privatization, and public debt during his first few years in office (Rubio and Goretti, 1998). Although this specific decree power was not explicitly contained in the 1853 [1949] Argentine Constitution, the Supreme Court validated its use in the 1990 case known as *Peralta* (Helmke 2005). Decree powers were subsequently adopted as part of the 1994 constitutional reforms.

Whereas scholars of the region have repeatedly voiced concern with the excessive reliance of presidents on their decree powers and leaders' seemingly endless thirst for power, Cox and Morgenstern (2002) were the first to clearly identify this as a particular presidential strategy, which presidents deploy in anticipation of facing what they term a "recalcitrant" Congress. In their view, these "imperial" presidents are vastly more likely to emerge when presidents either lack a congressional majority – through insufficient seats or party control – or lack the alternative means – through coalition building or through distributing pork – to cobble together a working majority.

But as we also know from the recent literature on presidential crises, presidents who follow this strategy do not necessarily always have the last word. Pérez-Liñán (2007) explicitly makes this point, citing numerous anecdotes of presidents who opted for a "strategy of isolation" and found themselves targeted for impeachment once the opportunity arose. For instance, in Fernando Collor de Mello's case, the Brazilian president had alienated Congress to such a degree that, by the time he was facing

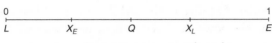

FIGURE 3.3: Bargaining over presidential power.

impeachment charges and sought to telephone legislators to ask for their support, a deputy reported thinking that the calls were a practical joke because Collor had never reached out to them before (Pérez-Liñán 2007: 152). More than two decades on, Dilma Rousseff appears to have repeated the same fundamental mistake. Of the recent Brazilian president's impeachment, the *New York Times* reported, "Many political analysts say Ms. Rousseff's slow-motion downfall can also be tied to an autocratic persona and a go-it-alone work style that has driven away scores of political allies, former staff members and cabinet ministers, many of whom have endured searing episodes of public humiliation."[6] Of course, precisely because legislatures do have the potential to sanction presidents who encroach on their powers, this brings us back to the original question of why these presidents fail to see the writing on the wall and adjust their behavior accordingly.

To supply an answer, consider the bargaining scenario depicted in Figure 3.3, due to Powell (1999). Here, I use the following notation: E represents the executive branch, L represents the congressional branch, Q represents the status quo distribution of the president's power to shape policies, X_E represents the president's offer, and X_L represents the legislature's counteroffer. Note that unlike standard spatial models, where each actor's utility improves as policy moves closer to his or her ideal point, the figure requires a different interpretation. Think of the distance between, say, the executive branch, E, and the status quo, Q, as the extent to which the president controls policymaking. Moving Q to the left expands the president's power; moving it to the right contracts it. The model is depicted in terms of the legislature's pie, whereby 1 implies that the legislature has total control over policy and 0 represents complete executive control over policy. For the ease of interpretation, the reversionary point for the legislature in the static model is 0.[7]

---

[6] Andrew Jacobs, "Dilma Rousseff, Facing Impeachment in Brazil, Has Alienated Many Allies," *New York Times*, May 1, 2016.

[7] In reality, legislatures do not necessarily lose everything by a failed impeachment. However, as long as the reversionary point is anywhere between 0 and Q, the following interpretation of the model remains the same.

Thus, consider X_E to be a proposal that the president might make to expand his or her power and X_L to be a proposal that the legislature might make to limit the president's power. Substantively, such proposals and counterproposals might range from the practical limitation or expansion of existing presidential powers to the actual rewriting of the constitutional rules. If we start with the executive's initial offer, then the legislature has the choice to accept the offer, propose an alternative (say, X_L), or embark on a punishment strategy, which effectively ends the game. Here, it is easiest to imagine the game-ending strategy as impeachment, though it could encompass any type of early presidential removal. If impeachment succeeds, then we assume that the legislature effectively captures the whole pie.[8]

The legislature's best response is derived by comparing its utilities over the various outcomes. Thus, imagine that the legislature is choosing between accepting the president's encroachment on the legislature's powers versus getting rid of the president. If the legislature accepts the president's proposal, then effectively it receives Q up until its acceptance of the president's proposal and X_E thereafter. Conversely, if the legislature decides to attempt to get rid of the president, its payoffs reflect both the probability that it may win, p, and thus gain control over the presidency, minus the costs of carrying out such an attack, d, plus the probability that it may fail, $1 - p$, minus the costs of carrying out such an attack, d. Intuitively, the legislature faces an incentive to attack whenever $p - d > Q$.

As such, the legislature's incentives for getting rid of the president depend on the relationship between these costs and benefits relative to the current distribution of policymaking power, or Q. To clarify this, consider Figure 3.4a, in which the legislature's payoff from attacking is still relatively small and X_E (and by extension Q) remains to the right of $p - d$. Here, the legislature has no incentive to challenge the president and the president can move policy to X_E. In Figure 3.4b, however, $p - d$ now falls in between Q and X_E, but as long as the president sticks with the status quo level of his policymaking powers, the legislature still does not have an incentive to attack. In Figure 3.4c, though, $p - d$ instead falls to the right of both X_E and Q, and the legislature now has an incentive to go after the president.

---

[8] Particularly in the Latin American context this assumption is not too far-fetched. As we saw from the previous chapter, the legislative opposition frequently replaces the ousted president with a leader of the opposition, which effectively means that the opposition now controls the entire policy-making pie.

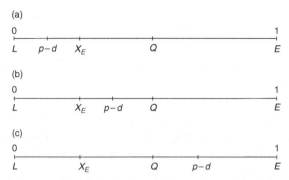

FIGURE 3.4: Bargaining in the shadow of a presidential crisis.

Several points flow from this. First, whereas in the simple crisis subgame contained in the previous section the president (qua Target) merely had the option to acquiesce to or fight impeachment after the attack was launched, here the president's decision over whether he should try to expand or limit his power in anticipation of sanctions is back in play. As such, the bargaining model sketched above reintroduces the fundamental question of why presidents do not strategically avert the threat by minimizing their policymaking powers ex ante. Under complete information, of course, it is easy to see that the foregoing setup dictates that as long as presidents know the legislature's payoffs, they should always make an offer that reflects the underlying distribution of partisan power. As Figure 3.5 shows, presidents should restrict their use of policymaking power to the point on the line at which E' is located.[9] Of course, were this the case, we would simply confirm our initial intuition that impeachment always remains strictly off the equilibrium path.

But if we operate instead under the arguably more realistic assumption that such scenarios are marked by asymmetric information, then presidential crises no longer remain a puzzle. To return to the figure above, if presidents do not know where precisely E' falls, then they cannot be sure how much power they can use and get away with. Consistent with Powell's (1999) line of reasoning, this presents presidents with a clear risk–return trade-off. The more policymaking control a president gives

---

[9] For a formal proof of this proposition, see Powell, 1999: 96–97.

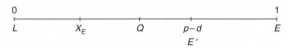

FIGURE 3.5: President's best response under complete information.

up, the more likely she is to satisfy the legislature, but also the more likely the president is to unnecessarily curtail her influence. Conversely, the less the president concedes, the more control she is able to exert, but the less likely she is to appease the legislature.[10]

Second, similar to the previous model, the size of the stakes again affects the threshold for fighting. In this case, however, it is the status quo allocation of constitutional power that drives the calculus, such that the more policymaking control the executive has (i.e., the farther Q is to the left), the lower the legislature's probability of success needs to be in order for it to face an incentive to attack. In the extreme, the strongest presidents imply that Q is pushed to a point where the legislature will face incentives to attack, even if the prospects for success are quite low. Conversely, it will take that much more for legislatures to be willing to attack relatively weak presidents. Indeed, at the other extreme, this theoretical framework suggests that weak presidents should be secure in office, even if they lack partisan support. In a nutshell, the higher the president's de jure powers are relative to the president's de facto powers, the greater the likelihood is for a bargaining problem to emerge. This leads to the first testable hypothesis.

H1 (Presidential Crises): The likelihood of a presidential crisis increases as the president's constitutional powers grow, conditional on the president's party being in the minority in the legislature.

At the same time, the model indicates that the cost to the legislature for going after the president should also make a difference in the legislature's calculus. All else equal, legislatures should be less willing to go after presidents when the costs for doing so are relatively high. In terms of

---

[10] Although above we have described uncertainty primarily in terms of presidential ambiguity over how many costs the legislature is willing to bear, note that uncertainty over the legislature's ability to succeed in forcing him from office will produce essentially the same dilemma for the president. In either event, the president is unable to formulate a precise understanding of how little or much he or she needs to give away in order to stay in power.

the core model, a higher d also effectively makes it more difficult for the legislature to overturn the status quo. As the following chapters describe in greater detail, costs can be operationalized in numerous ways, ranging from mass protests against the government to governmental scandals to public trust in the president and other institutions. For our purposes here, however, it is enough to simply specify the following hypothesis.

H2 (Presidential Crises): All else equal, the likelihood of a presidential crisis increases as the legislature's public costs for attacking the president decrease.

Taken together, the foregoing theoretical framework allows us to begin to make sense of the otherwise puzzling fact that Latin American presidents continue to push the envelope even when it would appear that prudence is the better choice. Ultimately, presidential crises depend on whether the president's offer is sufficient from the legislature's standpoint. But whether the offer is more or less likely to be sufficient takes us back to our initial observations about the legislature's calculus between the payoff it receives from sticking with the status quo distribution of policymaking power versus the payoff it gets from seeking to remove a president from power. Crucially, as we learned above, it is the gap between the president's constitutional powers, Q, and partisan powers, p, that provides the baseline condition for bargaining to fail. The fact that the president's lack of partisan support or fear of public approbation also inexorably pushes presidents to stretch their constitutional powers only sharpens the trade-off and opens the door further to attacks on the presidency.

3.4 SELF-COUPS AS A COMMITMENT PROBLEM: EXTENDING THE BARGAINING MODEL TO LEGISLATIVE CRISES

Thus far we have argued that the difference between the president's partisan and constitutional powers can help us to understand how institutional bargaining breaks down, thereby increasing the likelihood that a legislature will seek to force the sitting president out of office. But, of course, this is not the only type of institutional crisis that plagues Latin America. As we have seen, since the last wave of democratic transitions swept over the region, courts have been targeted roughly twice as often as executives. Legislatures have come under attack much less frequently than either branch, but when they have, the consequences for the constitutional order are arguably even worse. The goal of this section is thus to extend the insights of the foregoing bargaining model to develop a systematic account of why executives sometimes choose this "nuclear option." Below, I focus exclusively on legislative crises; Chapter 6 further expands this logic to explain how courts also get swept into the fray.

In keeping with our initial observations about the inherent differences among the branches, the answer, as we shall learn, does not lie simply in telling the inverse story. In other words, presidents who enjoy disproportionately more partisan powers than constitutional powers are not automatically tempted to upset the proverbial apple cart to grab power. The history of Mexican presidents throughout the second half of the twentieth century during the period of hegemony of the Institutional Revolutionary Party (PRI) provides an obvious case in point. As numerous Mexican experts have noted, institutionally the president was extremely weak, but because he enjoyed enormous partisan powers he was able to utterly dominate policymaking (Weldon, 1997; Magaloni, 2003). And, indeed, during that period in Mexican history executive-legislative relations were nothing if not stable.

Rather, to make sense of institutional attacks led by presidents requires making a different sort of modification to the original bargaining model. That is, we need to move from a static version of the bargaining framework, in which the threat a president faces is fixed, to a dynamic setting, in which the risk shifts over time. Extending further Powell's (1999) line of analysis to SOP systems, in this section I thus turn to explore how expected changes in the legislature's payoffs for launching a presidential crisis can serve to trigger legislative crises. For our purposes here, allowing this payoff to shift over time introduces two additional elements into the theoretical framework. First, it enables us to treat the dilemma that presidents face as a potential or future threat to their security. Second, by shifting the threat to the future, we open up an entirely new option for presidents beyond simply modifying their own powers: presidents can now effectively wage a preventive war against the legislature to avoid the future possibility of facing a Congress that is poised to remove them.

To elucidate how this dynamic works, imagine the previous three bargaining figures condensed onto a single line as shown in Figure 3.6, only now the legislature's payoffs for removing the president start at $(p - d)_1$ and change over four time periods $((p - d)_1, (p - d)_2, \ldots, (p - d)_4)$.

FIGURE 3.6: Dynamic bargaining in the shadow of a presidential crisis.

FIGURE 3.7: Bargaining in the shadow of changing de facto power with the option of a preventive strike.

As in the earlier model, note that the legislature still has no ability to credibly threaten the president with removal until its utility for doing so lies to the right of Q. Although the opposition's expected utility for getting rid of the president is growing between $(p - d)_1$ and $(p - d)_2$, that point is not effectively reached until $(p - d)_3$. Importantly, though, once this point is reached, the legislature cannot commit *not* to exploit its partisan powers to try to get the president to limit the use of his constitutional powers.

In turn, the fact that $p - d$ is shifting over time for the legislature now puts into play a new option for the president of launching a preventive strike at the outset. To see this, consider a situation in which the president's payoffs for attacking the legislature overlap with, but are not perfectly symmetrical with, the legislature's payoffs for attacking the president. Specifically, whereas the legislature's probability of success in ousting the president is conceptualized in terms of opposition seat share, the executive's probability of staging a successful legislative coup arguably depends more on the president's popularity, which is akin to d. Thus, I reconceptualize the parameter affecting the president's chance of success as d, where c represents a separate cost the president bears for transgressing the legislature's sovereignty.

Given these parameters, the executive's payoffs for staging a legislative crisis simplify to $d_1 - c = E''$, where capturing the pie effectively means moving Q (and p) all the way to the left and minimizing the legislature's payoff (and opposition seat share) to o.[11] Importantly, as long as the president's expected utility to staging a legislative crisis falls somewhere to the left of $(p - d)_4$, which we set here at E'', then the executive has an incentive to attack the legislature before conditions shift against him. Thus, even if the president's expected value from attacking the legislature makes the president worse off than sticking with the existing status quo

---

[11] Based on Figure 3.7, in which the executive is trying to minimize the legislature's share of the pie, the executive's payoff is calculated as follows: $d_1(1) + (1 - d_1)(0) - c = d_1 - c$, where 1 represents the policymaking pie which the executive controls with probability d_1, and o is the payoff for the executive for staging a legislative coup and failing. The o and 1 added below L and E represent the executive's payoffs.

(i.e., if C is sufficiently high, E'' lies to the right of Q), he should launch a preventive strike. With these payoffs in mind, we are now able to generate several novel testable implications for legislative crises.

The first hypothesis associated with legislative crises that flows out of the dynamic model again revolves around Q, or the president's constitutional powers. Similar to the core hypothesis for presidential crises, notice that the more Q moves to the left (i.e., the more the president's control of the policymaking pie expands), the less $p - d$ needs to shift for the legislature for the commitment problem to emerge. Put differently, because a higher Q makes it more likely that presidents will ultimately be at risk, it also creates the core conditions for a preventive legislative crisis under a minority president.[12] Thus, we get the following hypothesis.

H3 (Legislative Crises): The likelihood of a legislature being attacked increases as the president's constitutional powers grow, conditional on the president being in the minority.

Yet notice that the executive's payoff function for launching a legislative coup also admits an alternative, equally intuitive, mechanism. That is, simply the gap between the president's popularity and her constitutional powers relative to Q (i.e., $d - c > 1 - Q$) may provoke a legislative coup, regardless of the president's expectations about how the risks he faces in the future might shift. In this alternative narrative, a status quo distribution of constitutional powers toward the president actually decreases the probability of a legislative crisis; presidents are merely exploiting their popularity in order to grab more constitutional power. If this is the better explanation, then we would expect to find support for the proposition that presidential popularity among minority presidents conditions the negative effects of constitutional powers on legislative crises. As such, we get the fourth hypothesis.

H4 (Legislative Crises): Among minority presidents, the likelihood of a legislative crisis decreases with constitutional powers conditional on presidential popularity increasing.

---

[12] Note that according to a strict interpretation of the model, presidents should launch a preventive attack while they are in the majority. However, if a president already controls the legislature, there is obviously little need for a legislative coup. Empirically, moreover, there are almost no cases (less than 7%) in which majority presidents turn into minority presidents over the course of their terms, and vice versa. Rather, the more common pattern is for minority presidents to lose seats at midterm elections (see H6). This empirical regularity, combined with the fact that presidents can be removed from office only by a 50 percent threshold or higher, means that minority presidents are the most vulnerable to conditions shifting against them.

Returning to the preventive strike interpretation of the model, a third set of testable implications revolves explicitly around the president's expectations about how likely it is that he is going to be at risk during his administration. One factor potentially contributing to such beliefs is whether previous administrations have already been targeted by the legislature. Such experiences may help convince presidents at risk to negotiate and thus avoid being removed, but they also provide a road map for the opposition to oust the president, thus increasing p. Assuming the latter dominates the former, the following hypothesis emerges:

H5 (Legislative Crises): The likelihood of a legislative crisis increases with a history of previous attacks on presidents in a given country.

In the same vein, another plausible factor affecting the president's expectations is how dramatically the legislature's payoffs shift over time. In terms of the model, one scenario under which the president might expect that conditions will eventually shift against him would be if the balance of de facto power, p, is expected to change rapidly, say, a sudden shift from $(p - d)_1$ to $(p - d)_4$. For instance, the president may anticipate that she will lose seats in a nonconcurrent election, or expect that her coalition may suddenly collapse. Here, again, the president's recent predecessors' experience offers a plausible heuristic. In contexts where predecessors have rapidly lost partisan support, presidents should be more wary of being ousted than in contexts where previous presidents have not tended to lose seats over time. This can be stated as a testable hypothesis.

H6 (Legislative Crises): The likelihood of a legislative crisis increases with a history of predecessors losing partisan power over the course of their term in a given country.

With respect to the anticipated changes in the legislature's cost for attacking, d, the president is also likely to be attuned to how dramatically popular support for previous presidents has waxed and waned. This leads to the next hypothesis.

H7 (Legislative Crises): The likelihood of a legislative crisis increases with a history of predecessors losing popular support over the course of their term in a given country.

Likewise, we can also think about varying factors that raise the cost for presidents launching such an attack or that increase the probability of a successful legislative coup. Starting with the cost of violating the institutional order, the two following hypotheses articulate potential ways of

TABLE 3.1: *Summary of Hypotheses*

Parameters	Hypotheses
Q	H1, H3, H4
P	H1, H3, H5, H6, H10
d	H2, H4, H7, H10
c	H8, H9

capturing c. The first simply uses the legislature's popularity to gauge how costly it is for the president to launch a preventive strike. Thus, parallel to H2 is the following hypothesis.

H8 (**Legislative Crises**): The likelihood of a legislative crisis decreases as public support for the legislature increases.

The next implication builds on the observation that if parties constrain presidents, then stronger parties are arguably better poised to keep presidents in line because they have more to lose when the presidents alter the status quo. Hence we have the following hypothesis.

H9 (**Legislative Crises**): The likelihood of a legislative crisis increases as the strength of the president's party decreases.

The final testable implication involves timing. Of course, the very logic of acting preventively dictates that the president attempts to gain control over the other branches of government as soon as he or she can. In terms of the theory, we might imagine that if presidents are more likely to enjoy greater popularity at the beginning of their terms, then d will decrease over time. Conversely, to the extent that presidents tend to lose their seats in the midterm elections, then p is likely to grow over time. If either of these temporal trends exists, legislatures will be more likely to confront the commitment problem once the honeymoon period is over. To avoid this scenario, presidents should thus strike early in their terms, as per the next hypothesis.

H10 (**Legislative Crises**): The likelihood of a legislative crisis decreases with the amount of time the administration has been in power.

Table 3.1 summarizes how the four key parameters of the bargaining model map onto each of the ten hypotheses. The first, third, and fourth hypotheses explore how the distribution of formal constitutional powers affects the probability of both presidential crises and legislative crises. The first, third, fifth, sixth, and tenth hypotheses revolve around the president's current de facto powers (H_1, H_3) or the president's expectations about the future distribution of partisan support (H_5, H_6, H_{10}). As discussed above, the parameter d does double duty, both capturing the legislature's costs for instigating a presidential crisis (H_2, H_7, H_{10}) and serving as a proxy for the president's probability of carrying out a successful legislative coup (H_4, H_{10}). Finally, c represents the costs to the president for upsetting the institutional order and is captured by the eighth and ninth hypotheses.

3.5 CONCLUSION

In a well-functioning democracy institutional crises represent an anomaly. Given that men are not angels, checks and balances are necessary for making sure that one branch of government does not encroach on another or violate the rule of law. Yet, although it is tempting to conclude that all is well whenever guilty political actors are duly punished, the fact remains that institutions failed to prevent such behavior from occurring in the first place. Worse yet, we observe that checks and balances might instead be deployed opportunistically. Political actors may couch their actions in the language of anticorruption reforms or frame them as serving the broader national interest, but ultimately use whatever power they have to sanction or alter another branch of government in order to achieve partisan goals. Deciding which scenario best captures a particular institutional crisis is not always easy; indeed, in some instances it may be that sanctioning is well deserved, but still distorted for narrow political aims.

Leaving aside these sorts of normative debates about whether a given institutional clash is justified or not, this chapter has focused on developing the first unified theoretical account of the onset of institutional crises. To accomplish this, I have drawn on two sorts of off-the-shelf bargaining models of war. Such models provide a useful "engine of discovery" for understanding the dynamics of institutional crises.[13] Starting with a standard subcrisis game, I began by showing how a simple strategic theory of institutional instability helps unify several disparate insights within the existing literature.

Recognizing, however, that the specific dynamics of different types of inter-branch crises may not be entirely captured by this basic approach,

---

[13] I draw this phrase from Bates et al. (1998).

I then moved to a more flexible theoretical framework derived from Powell's (1999) seminal work on bargaining in the shadow of power. Using this as an analogue for understanding bargaining failures between the executive and legislative branches, I generated a series of novel, yet highly intuitive, observations linking the disparity between the president's partisan and constitutional powers to the onset of presidential and legislative crises. In a nutshell, I argued that because such disparity drives presidents to rule unilaterally, it also heightens the incentives of legislative opponents to get rid of such presidents. And yet precisely because legislative opponents cannot commit to forfeit their partisan powers to try to force such presidents from office, these leaders face their own incentives to try to preventively remove opponents within the legislature. The remaining chapters will evaluate how well this strategic bargaining account helps explain the patterns of institutional crises in contemporary Latin America.

4

Why the Mighty Fall

Explaining the Onset of Presidential Crises in Contemporary Latin America

Throughout most of the twentieth century, presidential instability in Latin America was synonymous with regime change. When elected leaders fell, so did democracy. Over the last few decades, however, this connection has been almost entirely broken.[1] Democracy in the region now endures, even as presidents are still routinely forced out of power. Argentina provides an obvious case in point. Between 1950 and 1983, the country earned the dubious distinction of having experienced more regime transitions than any other country in the world. But in 1989, despite suffering one of the worst bouts of hyperinflation in its history, President Alfonsín agreed to leave office early, and, for the first time in sixty years, power passed from one civilian administration to another. A decade later, with the economy again on the brink of disintegration, another Radical party president, Fernando de la Rúa, suddenly found his term cut short. The country then went on to witness no fewer than three presidents in the span of just two weeks, and yet democracy still survived (Levitsky 2005).

Struck by this new combination of governmental instability and regime stability, a growing number of scholars have sought to explain the onset of presidential crises in the absence of traditional military coups (Carey, 2003; Hinojosa and Pérez-Liñán, 2003; Valenzuela, 2004; Mainwaring and Pérez-Liñán, 2005; Hochstetler, 2006; Negretto, 2006; Pérez-Liñán, 2007; Kim and Bahry, 2008; Lehoucq, 2008; Hochstetler and Edwards, 2009; Llanos and Marsteintredet, 2010). In the main, this emerging

---

[1] Excluding Haiti, the three most frequently cited exceptions are Ecuador in 2000, Venezuela in 2002, and Honduras in 2010. In all three cases, the military was involved in removing the president, though civilians quickly took charge.

literature has found rather consistent evidence that mass protests and, to a somewhat lesser extent, scandals affect the likelihood of presidential removal. Surveying Latin America's recent string of failed presidencies, Valenzuela (2004) reflects on the "heat that the president and other officials can feel from protest movements seeking concrete solutions to real problems." Such protests, he adds, may begin over a specific griev-ance, but have an unfortunate tendency to snowball into a general demand for the government itself to go. In a similar vein, Hochstetler (2006) points out that mass protests by civil society actors have essentially taken on the moderating power role that used to be played by the military. When the masses demand that presidents are removed, she argues, legislative challenges to presidents tend to succeed; where only the legislature tries to remove the president, it often fails.[2]

Relatedly, scholars have also focused on the role played by scandals (Hochstetler, 2006; Pérez-Liñán, 2007; Kim and Bahry, 2008; Hochstetler and Edwards, 2009). Pérez-Liñán's (2007) careful study of presidential impeachments across Latin America finds substantial support for the claim that media scandals involving the president effectively drove down his public support.[3] In turn, scandals involving the administration appear to independently increase the probability that a president will, at the very least, be accused of wrongdoing by the legislature (Pérez-Liñán, 2007: 200; also see Hochstetler and Edwards, 2009: 49).

Importantly, the causal mechanism suggested by most of these accounts is entirely consistent with a central component of the model presented in the previous chapter. That is, societal factors matter, at least in part, because they affect the costs to legislatures for ousting presidents. To cite one familiar example, mass protests demanding President Collor's removal in the face of massive corruption charges allegedly played a pivotal role in pushing Brazilian legislators to act quickly and decisively to impeach the president, particularly in the context of looming midterm elections (Weyland, 1993; Hochstetler, 2006). In this instance, and in many others, whether routine inter-branch conflicts are ratcheted into full-fledged institutional crises depends on just how willing the public is to come to the president's

---

[2] Several quantitative analyses of interrupted presidencies confirm that mass protests sub-stantially increase the odds that a president will fall (Pérez-Liñán, 2007; Kim and Bahry, 2008; Álvarez and Marsteintredet, 2009; Hochstetler and Edwards, 2009).

[3] Pérez-Liñán also considers the reverse relationship. He finds strong preliminary evidence that if the president's popular approval is already in decline, the media are more likely to uncover corruption scandals involving the president (2007: 119–124).

defense or demand his ouster. The street matters, in short, precisely because it helps shapes elites' calculus about whether to oust presidents. To date, however, there is far less consensus within this growing body of empirical literature about the role of political institutions. Two points are especially worth noting. The first is that while nearly every recent study takes into account the president's partisan powers, very few explicitly consider the president's formal or constitutional powers. Second, whereas on balance most of these studies conclude that the president's partisan powers do affect his ability to maintain office,[4] there is little systematic support for the supposition that the distribution of formal institutional powers across branches of government fuels presidential ousters. Negretto (2006), for example, finds no evidence that whether presidents enjoy decree powers or face legislatures with the power to censure their cabinets has any impact on premature termination. Likewise, analyses by Kim and Bahry (2008) and Morgenstern, Negri, and Pérez-Liñán (2008) conclude that the extent of the president's formal legislative powers has no independent effect on whether powerful presidents are more prone to crises. Such findings are puzzling not only because they appear to run counter to the broader literature on presidentialism (Shugart and Carey, 1992; Jones, 1995; Archer and Shugart, 1997), but also because they clash with the insights of qualitative accounts regarding the deleterious effects of presidents ruling unilaterally (cf. Pérez-Liñán, 2007).

Building on the theoretical arguments developed in the previous chapter, this chapter reaches a very different set of conclusions. Whereas most quantitative analyses have considered the effects of partisan and formal powers only independently, or ignored the latter altogether, I demonstrate that the onset of presidential crises is instead driven by the interaction between the president's formal powers and his partisan status. As Chapter 3 argued, this stems from the basic observation that increasing the president's formal powers not only increases the president's incentives to go it alone (cf. Cox and Morgenstern, 2002), but also raises the opposition's incentives to try to replace him. If presidents do not know how

---

[4] Multiple studies have shown that minority presidents are more vulnerable (Valenzuela, 2004; Hochstetler, 2006; Hellwig and Samuels, 2007; Pérez-Liñán, 2007). In a similar vein, both Kim and Bahry (2008) and Ávarez and Marsteintredet (2009) find that the presidential share of seats is negatively related to presidential interruptions. Negretto (2004), however, argues that divided government is not sufficient for explaining presidential downfalls. Likewise, Hochstetler and Edwards (2009) find no statistical evidence that partisan support matters.

much power they need to cede to appease legislatures, then they confront an unfortunate, and often unsolvable, dilemma: foregoing more policy-making control may help presidents to stave off legislative attacks, but also may unduly limit their influence. The circumstances under which this dynamic unfolds, however, depend fundamentally on the president's partisan status. Simply put, if the president's party already controls Congress, there is no need for the president to rule around the legislature, nor for the legislature to try to get rid of the president. Under this scenario, increasing or diminishing the president's formal powers should essentially have no effect on the probability of crises. Conversely, when-ever the president lacks majority support, the bargaining model predicts that increasing the president's formal powers raises the probability that such a crisis will ensue.

To see this logic at work, compare Ecuador with Chile. Both countries are in the 90th percentile in terms of formal presidential powers, but the distribution of partisan support for the president varies dramatically from one country to the other. In Chile from 1990 until 2010, presidents came from the center-left coalition, Concertación, and essentially controlled the majority of the lower house seats. Since the coup that toppled Salvador Allende in 1973, not a single democratically elected president has been ousted. Now, consider Ecuador. With the partial exception of President Correa, over the last few decades no Ecuadorian president has even come close to controlling a majority of seats in the legislature. As a result, presidents in the 1980s and early 1990s were often forced to rely on so-called ghost coalitions in order to govern (Mejia Acosta, 2006, 2009). Unlike Chile, such postelectoral coalitions proved fleeting and unstable, as illustrated in 1996 by the defection of the Social Christian Party (PSC) from Durán-Ballén's government and the subsequent ouster of his vice president, Alberto Dahik. Meanwhile, the very institutional reforms that further increased presidential powers in the late 1990s severely under-mined the president's ability to sustain such coalitions (Mejía Acosta and Polga-Hecimovich, 2010). Given this fateful combination, the massive wave of institutional instability that swept over Ecuador's minority presi-dents from 1997 until 2006 is entirely in keeping with the general theor-etical perspective advanced in this book.

The fundamental question taken up in the rest of this chapter is whether the sort of pattern exemplified by Chile and Ecuador is borne out in a broader systematic analysis. Using the original ICLA dataset described in Chapter 2, the remainder of this chapter conducts a series of statistical tests aimed at evaluating my argument and comparing it with previous approaches. Following a description of the variables used in the analysis, I begin by replicating the standard finding that simply accounting for formal constitutional powers has little impact on the likelihood of a presidential crisis. Using this as a baseline, I then show not only that a strong interaction effect exists between minority presidents and their constitutional powers, but also that my model best fits the empirical data. To ensure that these results do not hinge on any specific estimation strategy or operationalization of the key independent variables, I perform six types of robustness checks. Along the way, I also discuss the handful of cases that are incorrectly predicted by the core interactive model, thus paving the way for additional insights into the logic of presidential crises.

4.1 THE DATA

To test the core predictions that flow from my theoretical model regarding the onset of presidential crises, this chapter draws on a subset of the ICLA dataset. As discussed in Chapter 2, the data cover eighteen Latin America countries (Argentina, Bolivia, Brazil, Chile, Colombia, Costa Rica, the Dominican Republic, Ecuador, El Salvador, Guatemala, Honduras, Mexico, Nicaragua, Panama, Paraguay, Peru, Venezuela, and Paraguay) between 1985 (or the first year the country enters the data set as a democracy) and 2008. Because this chapter focuses exclusively on predicting the onset of presidential crises, I consider only those observations in which the ordered-dyad is the legislature-executive. Thus, the total number of observations is 474. The next section describes how the various dependent and independent variables used in the analysis are measured.

4.1.1 Dependent Variables

As Chapter 2 elaborated, analyzing properly the onset of inter-branch crises requires taking into account all cases in which crises occur and comparing them with all instances in which they do not occur. Moreover, because my theoretical framework is focused more generally on the onset of presidential crises, not necessarily on their resolution, I treat all instances in which Congress attempted to remove the president as a presidential crisis, regardless of whether they succeeded or failed in getting rid of the president. *Presidential Crises* are thus coded as 1 if the legislature threatened or succeeded in impeaching or otherwise

TABLE 4.1: *Presidential Crises*

Successful Removal	Attempted Removal
Argentina 2001	Bolivia 1990
Bolivia 1985, 2003	Brazil 1999, 2005
Brazil 1987, 1992	Colombia 1995, 2000
Dominican Republic 1994	Ecuador 1987, 1990, 1992, 1995, 2004, 2005, 2007
Ecuador 1997, 1999, 2005	Nicaragua 1995, 1997, 2004, 2005, 2007
Guatemala 1993	Paraguay 1996, 2001, 2002, 2005
Paraguay 1998	Peru 1991
Peru 2000	Venezuela 2002
Venezuela 1992	

removing the president from office during a given administration- year. This measure effectively picks up the thirteen episodes from 1985 to 2008 in which presidents have been successfully removed from office early by the legislature, as well as twenty-three instances during this period in which presidents faced a threat of removal from Congress, but managed to remain in office (see Table 4.1). All administration-years in which the president did not face such a challenge from the legislature are coded as 0.

Of course, not all legislatures have necessarily played an equally influential role across the various cases of presidential removal (cf. Hochstetler, 2006; Pérez-Liñán, 2007; Hochstetler and Edwards, 2009; Mustapic, 2010). In some instances, specifically the Dominican Republic (1994), Ecuador (1999), Peru (2000), Argentina (2001), and Bolivia (2003), legislators were primarily reacting to exogenous events that had already occurred. In the Dominican Republic, the legislature played only a very peripheral role in shortening Balaguer's term following his fraudulent election (Marsteintredet, 2010). In the case of Ecuador, the Congress merely declared that President Mahuad had abandoned his post after he was effectively unseated by indigenous protesters and a coup carried out by Colonel Lucio Gutiérrez. Likewise, in Fujimori's case the Peruvian legislature impeached the president on grounds of "moral incapacity" after he had already fled the country. In Argentina, Peronist legislators raised the possibility of impeaching de la Rúa only after the economy had spiraled out of control and protesters had been killed; and, of course, de la Rúa resigned before the legislature could make much headway on its threat (although see Llanos and Marsteintredet, 2010: 64). The same is largely true of Sánchez de Lozada's ouster in Bolivia two years later. To address these differences,

I construct an alternative measure, *Presidential Crisis_Limited*, which excludes the five foregoing cases and effectively limits the dependent variable to include only those cases in which the legislature played a substantial role in removing the executive from power. In addition, to deal with the possibility that some of the threats that failed to come to fruition may not have been equally credible, I construct a second alternative measure, *Presidential Crisis_Success*, which focuses exclusively on the thirteen cases in which presidents were successfully removed by their legislatures.

4.1.2 Independent Variables

To evaluate the previous chapter's core prediction that the interaction between the president's constitutional legislative powers and partisan support fuels presidential crises, I develop separate measures for each component and an interaction term based on these measures. In addition, we also need to develop a systematic way to measure the costs that such removals entail for the legislature. Below, I describe the variety of ways in which each of the key theoretical concepts is operationalized for the purposes of exploring the model's central propositions.

Constitutional Powers

Let me start with the president's constitutional powers. Specifically, the model requires a measure that captures the extent to which presidents are able to shape policy outcomes over the heads of the legislature. To date, however, the emerging literature on presidential crises has relied on indicators that do not adequately represent this type of presidential power. For instance, Kim and Bahry (2008) employ the commonly used executive constraints (XCONST) measure from Polity IV, which includes the very sorts of executive and legislative behavioral outcomes that we want to predict.[5] They also use a second measure of presidential power developed by Siaroff (2003), which takes us more in the direction of gauging the president's institutional powers (i.e., whether presidents have veto power or decree power), but also includes a number of additional factors (e.g., whether presidents are elected and whether legislative and presidential elections are concurrent) that are well outside the scope of the

---

[5] For instance, XCONST also considers whether or not the executive frequently rules by decree, whether the constitution is frequently revised or suspended at the executive's initiative, and whether constitutional restrictions on executive action are ignored.

parameter we are trying to capture.[6] Conversely, Negretto (2006) focuses solely on whether presidents have decree power and/or legislatures can censure the president's cabinets, thus ignoring the multitude of other institutional features described below that also allow presidents to shape policy.[7]

Fortunately, building on Shugart and Carey's (1992) seminal work on presidentialist systems, other scholars have a developed a complete list of formal institutional indicators to measure the full range of the president's legislative powers. Obviously, there is still some slippage between the president's formal constitutional powers and his actual legislative powers, but this hardly invalidates the supposition that the president's formal legislative powers provide a good indicator of his ability to shape policy outcomes (Shugart and Carey, 1992). Here, I construct measures of the constitutional powers of presidents gathered by Alemán and Tsebelis (2005), Mainwaring and Shugart (1997), and Negretto (2014).

The first measure of formal presidential power draws on the cross-national indicators developed by Alemán and Tsebelis (2005), which updates the original Shugart and Carey (1992) measures and yields one of the most comprehensive available cross-national indices of the president's formal powers. Altogether, they consider twelve separate factors pertaining to the institutional authority of presidents in eighteen Latin American countries.[8] *Presidential Power* is thus constructed as an aggregate measure of these twelve indicators, which ranges from a low score of 18 for Mexico, a country widely considered to have one of the weakest constitutional presidencies (cf. Weldon, 1997), to a high score of 33 for Ecuador, a country commonly viewed as having one of the strongest constitutional presidencies in Latin America (cf. Mainwaring and Shugart, 1997). The variable is then rescaled from 1 to 16.

Given recent methodological critiques of aggregate indices (Olmsted et al., 2015), I also explore both fully disaggregated versions of this measure (i.e., a model that includes each factor as well as each factor interacted with minority government) and partially aggregated

---

[6] Moreover, despite the broad nature of Siaroff's measures, there is actually remarkably little variation across Latin American presidencies.

[7] In addition, there are several studies that focus specifically on the president's decree powers (Carey and Shugart, 1998; Negretto, 2004; Pereira, Power and Renno, 2005).

[8] Such factors include presidential control over financial legislation, the ability of presidents to compel attention to urgent bills and unilaterally call special sessions of Congress, various veto-related and decree procedures, and the ability of the president to shape policy through referenda.

component-based measures that are drawn from Alemán and Tsebelis' original conceptual framework, which groups the original twelve indicators into four categories: financial legislation, bill shaping powers, proactive powers, and reactive powers.

To check the robustness of my results, I also employ the original measure of constitutional presidential powers for Latin America, *Presidential Power_SM*, which is based on a four-fold typology developed by Mainwaring and Shugart (1997). Their typology rests exclusively on reactive and proactive presidential powers. Reactive powers (e.g., veto, partial veto, exclusive introduction of bills) thus allow the president to maintain the legislative status quo; proactive powers (e.g., nonregulatory decree powers) instead enable him or her to unilaterally change the status quo. Based on their assumption that proactive powers are more important than reactive powers, they create the following four types of presidents: (1) potentially dominant presidents, who enjoy both types of power; (2) proactive presidents, who have decree powers, but a relatively weak veto; (3) reactive presidents, who have a strong veto, but no decree powers; and (4) potentially marginal presidents, who have neither a strong veto nor any decree powers. The variable *Presidential Power_SM* is constructed by scoring these types numerically from 4 to 1. Compared with the Alemán and Tsebelis original index, Shugart and Mainwaring thus focus on a smaller set of institutional factors. The overall correlation between the Alemán and Tsebelis measure and *Presidential Power_SM* is 0.73.

One potential shortcoming of using either Alemán and Tsebelis' or Shugart and Mainwaring's data, however, is that the measures they report are purely cross-sectional, representing each country's constitutional system at a certain point in time (i.e., 2005 and 1997, respectively). For my purposes, this potentially presents a problem if (1) a country has changed its constitution at some point during the period under analysis (1985–2008) and (2) it has done so in such a way that alters the fundamental balance of executive-legislative power. According to data recently compiled by Negretto (2014), the following countries reformed or rewrote their constitutions at least once between 1985 and 2008: Argentina (1994), Bolivia (1995), Brazil (1988 and 2001), Colombia (1991), Chile (1989 and 1997), Ecuador (1998 and 2008), Nicaragua (1987, 1995, and 2000), Paraguay (1992), Peru (1993), Uruguay (1997), and Venezuela (1999). The overall temporal trend has been to strengthen the president's agenda-setting legislative powers, though in a handful of cases some of the president's legislative powers were reduced (Brazil 1988 and 2001, Colombia 1991, Nicaragua 1987,

Paraguay 1992). Thus, I use Negretto's measures of president's legislative powers as a second alternative measure.[9]

Although there is substantial overlap between the institutional factors coded by Negretto (2014) and Alemán and Tsebelis (2005), the measures are not identical. In addition to the scales having different ranges, Negretto does not include a measure of participation in plenary debate, and Alemán and Tsebelis do not include a separate measure for decree outcome. Nevertheless, the correlations across the main components (financial legislation, shaping power, proactive power, and reactive power) are relatively high. Specifically, if I restrict Negretto's data to the year 2005, the correlations between the Alemán and Tsebelis' components and Negretto's range from 0.68 to 0.76. Not surprisingly, the correlations between Alemán and Tsebelis and the Negretto time-series data are much lower, ranging from 0.46 to 0.68.[10]

Partisan Powers

In the broader literature on presidentialism, the president's partisan powers are based on several factors, including the number of seats the president's party holds in Congress, the effective number of parties, the level of party discipline and party cohesion, and the degree of ideological polarization (e.g., see Mainwaring, 1993; Jones, 1995; Mainwaring and Shugart 1997; Morgenstern and Nacif 2002). Each of these affects the president's ability to forge coalitions and govern effectively, and each, in turn, is a product of a variety of institutional rules. Thus, the party system stems, at least in part, from the specific electoral formula and/or the district magnitude, as well as election timing or sequencing (Duverger 1954; Cox 1997; Mainwaring and Shugart 1997). Party discipline, cohesion, and ideological polarization are the product of ballot structure, party control over nominations, the size of the assembly, and federalism (Shugart and Carey, 1992; Morgenstern and Nacif, 2002).

The question that most concerns us here, however, is not why or how the president's partisan powers originate, but how to best operationalize the president's partisan support in terms of her ability to thwart a

---

[9] The data can be found at: http://la-constitutionalchange.cide.edu/en/data

[10] The correlation between the measures used by Alemán and Tsebelis (2005) and Negretto (2014) restricted to 2005 are as follows: Financial Legislation = 0.75, Shaping Bills Power = 0.68, Reactive Power = 0.76, Proactive Power = 0.74. The correlation between the measures used by Alemán and Tsebelis (2005) and Negretto's time-series cross-sectional data (2014) are as follows: Financial Legislation = 0.60, Shaping Bills Power = 0.68, Reactive Power = 0.63, Proactive Power = 0.46.

congressional attempt at removal. Specifically, to test the model developed in the previous chapter requires creating a measure of the parameter, p, which refers to the probability that the legislature will be able to successfully carry out an attack against the executive branch. To accomplish this, I begin by employing a dummy variable, *Minority President*, which indicates whether or not the president's party lacks the majority of seats in the lower chamber of Congress.[11] Although relatively crude, the main virtue of this measure is that it avoids many of the ambiguities associated with several of the other variables listed above. For instance, consider the potential problems associated with using the effective number of parties to capture the president's ability to thwart a legislative attack. First, if the effective number of parties is treated primarily as a predictor of minority government (Mainwaring, 1993; Mainwaring and Shugart, 1997), why not simply use a direct measure of the status of the government? Moreover, it is not entirely clear that a system with several parties is automatically worse for minority presidents than, say, a system with three evenly matched parties (cf. Cheibub, 2002; Negretto, 2006). After all, and as I will discuss more fully below, the more parties there are in the opposition, the greater the collective action problem the opposition faces in trying to remove the president (cf. Morgenstern, Negri, and Pérez-Liñán, 2008).

Likewise, it is important to recognize that when it comes to averting presidential crises, party discipline and cohesion can cut both ways. Depending on the scenario, presidents facing the threat of removal will obviously be hurt by the lack of discipline or factions within their own party, but can potentially benefit from weaker party discipline among the opposition. And while coalitions are often vital for determining whether minority presidents are able to effectively govern, their notorious fragility

---

[11] Using a dichotomous variable allows me to capture the fact that the threat to the president is largely discontinuous. In other words, under most institutional rules (see below), the difference between a president who has 49 percent of the seats and one who has 51 percent is far greater than the difference between a president who controls 20 percent versus 25 percent of the seats. To calculate the president's minority status in the lower house, I gathered electoral data for each administration country year from the following sources: the 2006 Database of Political Institutions Worldbank dataset, Georgetown University's Center for Latin American Studies' Political Database of the Americas (PDBA), Binghamton University's Center on Democratic Performance's Election Results Archive (ERA), Psephos Election Archive, and various Wikipedia country-election pages. Data from McDonald and Ruhl (1989) were used to fill in missing information for the following administrations: Ortega (Nicaragua, first administration), Sanguinetti (Uruguay), Cordova (Honduras), and Siles Zuazo (Bolivia).

means that such alliances are themselves potentially endogenous to presidential crises – a lesson that leaders such as Brazil's Fernando Collor de Mello, Bolivia's Hernán Siles Zuazo, and Ecuador's Jamil Mahuad learned the hard way. For all of these reasons then, whether or not the president's party holds the minority of seats arguably provides the clearest and cleanest starting point for assessing the potential legislative threat.

As it happens, using a simple minority measure also serves as a relatively good indicator of Pérez-Liñán's (2007) more nuanced concept of the president's "legislative shield." In its most basic formulation, the size of the legislative shield is the difference between the percentage of seats controlled by the president's party and the institutional threshold required for initiating procedures to impeach or otherwise remove the president from office. Thus, if two-thirds of the lower chamber is constitutionally required to initiate impeachment proceedings, the president does not need to control a majority of seats to weather a crisis; he is shielded as long as he controls just over a third of the seats.

Theoretically, of course, this suggests that focusing exclusively on whether the president lacks majority control potentially overestimates the legislature's ability to remove the president. Empirically, however, data compiled by Pérez-Liñán (2007: 140–141) reveal that the vast majority of Latin American constitutions contain provisions that enable a simple majority to initiate impeachment[12] or allow for a declaration of presidential incapacity.[13] As a result, it turns out that for roughly two-thirds of the data (twelve of eighteen countries), the variable *Minority President* is essentially equivalent to employing a dummy variable that captures whether the president has a legislative shield. That said, to account for countries or periods in a country's history for which majority status does not accurately capture whether the president has a legislative shield, I construct a second variable, *Shield*, which recalculates the status of the president's partisan support according to the exact institutional threshold.[14]

---

[12] Bolivia (1967–1994), Chile (1980), Colombia (1886 [1991]), El Salvador (1983), Honduras (1982), Mexico (1917), Nicaragua (1995–2000), Peru (1979 [1993]), Uruguay (1997).

[13] Costa Rica (1949) and Ecuador (1978 [1998]).

[14] According to data collected by Pérez-Liñán (2007: 140–141) on constitutional rules on impeachment and the declaration of incapacity in Latin America, the following countries have a lower bar (34%) for blocking the removal of the president: Argentina (1853 [1994]), Brazil (1988), Guatemala (1985), Panama (1972), Paraguay (1992). In the Dominican Republic (1966 [1994, 2002]), 26 percent can block removal.

As I hinted above, one obvious remaining concern in measuring partisan support is that not all minority government situations are necessarily equivalent in terms of the threat they pose to presidents. Some oppositions are strong and united; others are weak and divided (Negretto, 2006; Morgenstern, Negri and Pérez-Liñán, 2008). All else equal, we would expect the latter to have a more difficult time mustering the support needed to remove a sitting president, and that it would be significantly more challenging for the opposition to agree to a replacement. The uneasy alliance between Arnoldo Alemán's Liberals and Daniel Ortega's Sandinistas under Enrique Bolaños' government offers a case in point. Throughout 2004 and 2005 Bolaños' administration teetered on the brink of crisis under threat from the pact between the Constitutionalist Liberal Party (PLC) and the Sandinista National Liberation Front (FSLN). Removing the president from office, however, would have brought a key ally of Alemán's to power, which ultimately proved to be anathema to the Sandinistas.[15] As a result, Bolaños was ultimately able to strike a deal with Ortega, thus allowing the president to remain in power until the end of his term.[16]

To address these sorts of issues systematically, here I develop a second alternative measure of partisan support, *Minority Situation*, which draws on Negretto's (2006) classification that takes into account both the president's seat share and the president's policy position relative to the other parties. Using a one-dimensional spatial model, Negretto (2006) persuasively argues that minority presidents confront a much more difficult situation whenever their parties do not occupy the ideological center and thus fail to control either the median or veto legislator or both. This allows us to distinguish situations in which the minority presidents face a weak and/or divided opposition ("unified" and "median" governments) from situations in which they confront a united and powerful opposition (e.g., "divided" and "congressional" governments). In terms of my model, minority presidents should have a distinct advantage in averting attacks whenever the opposition stands to the left or right of the president.

Costs

According to my theoretical model, legislatures should also be sensitive to the costs of launching a presidential crisis. Here, following the existing

---

[15] According to reports, Vice President José Rizo was a personal friend of Arnoldo Alemán (*LAWR*), December 7, 2004).

[16] *LAWR*, October 25, 2005.

literature, I conceptualize costs largely in terms of the public's willingness to oppose or support the legislature's attempts to remove the president. Intuitively, as the costs to seeking the president's removal rise, legislatures should be less willing to initiate an inter-branch crisis. The failure of the so-called tentative coup against the highly popular Ecuadorian President Rafael Correa in September 2010 offers a perfect illustration.[17] Conversely, should a president lose public favor, the legislature will have a much greater ability to move forward and, in fact, may face heavy popular pressures to do so. Along these lines, just seven months after President Abdalá Bucaram's inauguration, mass protests and plummeting approval ratings infamously spurred a majority of the Ecuadorian legislature to resort to charges of mental incapacity to remove Bucaram from office (Pérez-Liñán, 2007: 106–109; Mejía Acosta and Polga-Hecimovich, 2010: 81–82). Likewise, in Brazil in 2016, mounting protests demanding "fora Dilma" led an equally discredited legislature to vote for her impeachment.[18]

Building on the existing literature on presidential crises, here I employ three separate measures to capture the costs to the legislature: *Protests, Scandals,* and *Public Support.* The first of these measures comes from data gathered by Banks (2005), which documents the number of anti-governmental demonstrations for each country per year. This measure has also been used in previous quantitative analyses on presidential crises conducted by Kim and Bahry (2008) and Álvarez and Marsteintredet (2009). Of course, not all antigovernmental protests are alike. As the ousters of de la Rúa in Argentina and Sánchez de Lozada in Bolivia attest, demonstrations that end in violence are particularly problematic for sitting presidents (Valenzuela, 2004; Hochstetler, 2006). Yet, as the series of failed presidencies in Ecuador suggests, even demonstrations that do not end in bloodshed can help convince elites in Congress that the administration has lost control over events and needs to be replaced (Mejía Acosta and Polga-Hecimovich, 2010). Thus, for our purposes here, antigovernmental demonstrations offer a rough but clear proxy of the potential costs that legislatures face in seeking to get rid of sitting presidents.

---

[17] The phrase "tentative coup" was used by the Organization of American States Secretary General José Miguel Insulza in his address about the coup to Inter-American Dialogue, Washington, DC, October 21, 2010.

[18] Andrew Jacobs,, April 17, 2016, "Brazil's Lower House of Congress Votes for Impeachment of Dilma Rousseff" (www.nytimes.com/2016/04/18/world/americas/brazil-dilma-rousseff-impeachment-vote.html?_r=0).

The second measure, *Scandals*, due to Hochstetler (2006), is based on incidents of reported corruption or other types of personal scandals involving the president (2006: 407; for a similar measure, see Pérez-Liñán, 2007). As discussed above, previous scholarship finds that political scandals both severely erode public support for the president and/or fuel mass protests. Whether or not they directly translate into presidential removal, however, is less clear. For instance, although scandals do seem to increase the probability that the legislature accuses the president of misdeeds, they also can produce a kind of rally-around-the-flag effect whereby legislators are actually less likely to vote to oust a president (Pérez-Liñán, 2007: 174). Ultimately, this may explain why Pérez-Liñán (2007) and Kim and Bahry (2008) do not uncover any significant direct impact of scandals on the likelihood that presidents will be successfully removed from power; whereas Hochstetler and Edwards (2009) find that once we take the initial challenge into account, scandals actually slightly decrease the likelihood that the president will be ousted. Here, however, I use scandals simply as an alternative measure for costs that helps predict the onset of presidential crises, not their particular resolution.

The third measure, *Presidential Confidence*, draws on public opinion data contained in the Latinobarómetro (1995–2007). Latinobarómetro includes a series of survey questions asking citizens how much confidence or trust they have in each of the three branches of government ("a lot," "some," "little," or "none"). Using these data for the executive branch, I generate average support scores lagged by one year for each observation.[19] Importantly, despite the common view that institutions in Latin America are universally weak and distrusted, there is considerable variation in public trust across countries and over time. For instance, in Argentina during the 2002 economic crises just 7 percent of people reported having "a lot" or even "some" trust in the executive branch. By contrast, fully 71 percent of Peruvians expressed confidence in Fujimori during his successful bid for a second term in 1995.[20]

---

[19] Average scores are generated by multiplying the percentage of respondents in each category and then adding them together as follows: "A Lot" $\times$ 2 + "Some" $\times$ 1 + "A Little" $\times$ −1 + "None" $\times$ −2.

[20] Although the Latinobarómetro provides the most comprehensive single source for cross-national public opinion data for this period, the annual surveys are not available prior to 1995, nor for the year 1999. In addition, not all countries have been included in the surveys since 1995. For instance, Bolivia and Honduras are not included by Latinobarómetro until 1997; the Dominican Republic is not included until 2004. All told, there are

Economic and Instability Controls

Previous cross-national analyses of presidential crises have found rather consistent results regarding the impact of various economic factors. Most authors, for instance, find that inflation has no effect on whether presidents fall, but that economic recession/growth significantly raises/lowers the odds of presidential interruption (Kim and Bahry 2008; Álvarez and Marsteintredet 2009; Hochstetler and Edwards 2009). Likewise, most cross-national studies conclude that gross domestic product (GDP) has a negative effect on crises.[21] To control for these factors in my analysis, I thus include annual measures for *GDP*, *Growth*, *Inflation*, and *Unemployment* from data drawn from the World Development Indicators (WDI) database. Finally, to address the question of whether countries have different propensities for institutional instability more generally that are due to unobserved characteristics, I also construct a simple count measure of previous regime transitions using the Przeworski et al. (2000) data.

4.2 EMPIRICAL ANALYSIS AND RESULTS

Whereas the recent quantitative literature has deemed that formal presidential powers are largely irrelevant for explaining the onset of presidential crisis, the bargaining model presented in the previous chapter instead posits that the president's formal legislative powers do matter, but only for minority presidents. Which account finds more empirical support? To begin to answer this question, this section compares the standard multivariate model of presidential crisis with an interactive model. After demonstrating that the interactive model best fits the data, I then show substantively the effects of this interaction on the probability of crises. In addition, I demonstrate that while the vast bulk of cases is correctly predicted by the core interactive model, I also suggest that a closer examination of specific cases that are incorrectly predicted also roughly fits with the theoretical story. Finally, I assess the robustness of my results by rerunning my analyses with a slew of alternative measures for each of the key variables. Because the distribution of crises relative to noncrises in the data is relatively unbalanced, (36 of 474 crises, or just

survey data for 920 of the 1,896 observations contained in the ICLA dataset, or for only roughly half of all observations.

[21] Note that Pérez-Liñán (2007) looks at the impact of economic factors on presidential crises indirectly, assessing the effect of inflation and unemployment on protest.

8 percent of all observations), I correct for the underestimation of event probabilities by estimating rare events logit models throughout.[22] I cluster the data by country given that certain unspecified country attributes may not vary across administrations.

4.2.1 Model Testing and Nested Comparisons

Let me start with the conventional multivariate model of presidential crises seen in Model 4.1 (without controls) and Model 4.2 (with controls). Replicating the existing literature's findings, Model 4.1 shows that both of the coefficients for *Minority President* and *Protests* are positive and statistically significant, whereas the coefficient that captures constitutional powers, *Presidential Power*, is statistically insignificant. In other words, in line with the previous literature's conclusions, partisan and societal factors appear to determine the president's fate; the president's formal constitutional powers do not seem to matter. Although as soon as economic controls are added (Model 4.2), notice that the purported effects for minority presidents also disappear.

Now, consider columns 3 and 4 of Table 4.2, in which the interaction term, *Minority x Power*, takes on the value of the president's formal constitutional powers for minority presidents and zero otherwise. Fully in line with the book's main argument, the interaction terms in both models are positive and statistically significant, indicating that the odds that a minority president will be challenged indeed increase as the president's formal legislative powers increase, whether we control for economic factors or not.[23] The coefficients for the interaction variable's two constituent terms, *Minority President* and *Presidential Power*, reflect the impact of each variable when the other is held at zero (Brambor, Clark, and Golder, 2006). The fact that neither of these terms is significant in Model 4.3 or Model 4.4 further bolsters the corollary theoretical expectation that there is no effect of

---

[22] I set prior correction to .07594937 to reflect the complete sample, and use *nomcn* to suppress the sampling correction (by default, ReLogit corrects for sampling on dependent variable). See King and Zeng (2001) and Tomz, King, and Zeng (2003). Note that although the structure of the complete ICLA dataset allows for conditional-nested logit, this is not the appropriate research design given my theoretical framework.

[23] Because nearly a third of presidential crises occur in Ecuador, it would be surprising if the results survived dropping Ecuador entirely from the sample. Thus, I reran the core model dropping the Ecuadorian administrations one by one; ultimately, the results are robust to dropping seven of the ten crises in Ecuador.

TABLE 4.2: *Contrasting the Standard Model of Presidential Crises with the Interactive Model*

	(Model 4.1) Standard Model	(Model 4.2) Standard with Controls	(Model 4.3) Core Interactive Model	(Model 4.4) Interactive with Controls
Minority President	1.06** (0.53)	0.76 (0.62)	−0.84 (0.93)	−1.68 (1.23)
Presidential Power	0.10 (0.07)	0.12 (0.09)	−0.11 (0.10)	−0.11 (0.10)
Minority × Power			0.24** (0.11)	0.29** (0.12)
Protest	0.32*** (0.08)	0.29*** (0.08)	0.33*** (0.08)	0.27*** (0.10)
GDP		0.08 (0.11)		0.12 (0.12)
Growth		−0.06 (0.04)		−0.05 (0.04)
Inflation		0.05 (0.11)		0.05 (0.12)
Unemployment		0.04 (0.04)		0.05 (0.04)
Constant	−4.56*** (1.02)	−4.85*** (1.27)	−3.01*** (0.96)	−3.11** (1.22)
N	454	392	454	392

* $p < 0.1$,
** $p < 0.05$,
*** $p < 0.01$.

increasing presidential powers when presidents are in the majority and there is no effect of being a minority president when presidents lack substantial constitutional powers. Finally, in both models, *Protests* continues to exert a positive influence on the likelihood of crisis, which again fits nicely with the theoretical expectation that legislatures are sensitive to the potential public costs for removing presidents.

A simple Wald test helps to determine whether the conventional or the core model best fits the data. Specifically, I evaluate the significance of including the interaction term from the basic interactive model (Model 4.3) compared with the conventional multivariate model (Model 4.1). At 0.02, the *p*-value indicates that including the interaction term indeed improves significantly the fit of the model. As a result, we can conclude that, although both the standard and the interactive models contain independent variables with explanatory power, the latter does a better job.

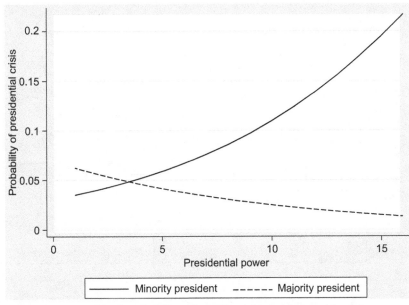

FIGURE 4.1: Predicted probability of presidential crises by presidential power among minority and majority presidents.

4.2.2 Assessing Substantive Effects

Based on the results of the core interactive model, Figure 4.1 shows the predicted probabilities of the president's formal constitutional powers on the likelihood of crisis for minority presidents (solid line) and majority presidents (dashed line), respectively. In accordance with our main theoretical story, we see that increasing the president's formal constitutional powers substantially increases the odds of a presidential crisis, from approximately 0.03, when presidential power is at its weakest, to 0.22, when presidential power is at its strongest. But, again, the effect is present only for presidents who are in the minority.

Next, Figure 4.2 plots the marginal effects, showing the impact of minority versus majority presidents on presidential crises for different levels of presidential power. Note that the dashed lines, which represent the lower and upper bounds of the 95 percent confidence intervals, respectively, are both above the zero line only once presidential power is sufficiently high, at roughly scores of 6 or higher.[24] This means that the

---

[24] Countries that score 6 or higher on the presidential power scale include Argentina, 8; Brazil, 6; Bolivia, 8; Colombia, 11; Costa Rica, 7; Chile, 13; Ecuador, 16; Guatemala, 6;

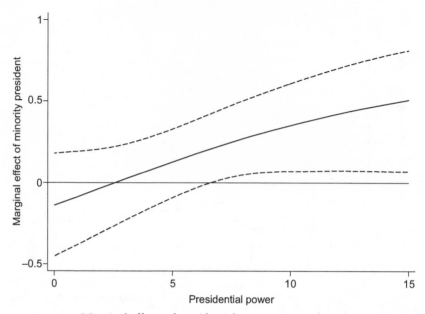

FIGURE 4.2: Marginal effects of presidential power on presidential crises among minority presidents.

marginal effect of being in the minority is statistically significant for the vast majority of observations in the dataset.

Next, to see how well the interactive model fits the observed data at the administration level, I calculate the observed and predicted values for the dependent variable. Using the 80th percentile as the threshold for a predicted crisis, Table 4.3 shows that the model overall predicts 77 percent of the cases correctly. What, if anything, can we discern from the cases that are incorrectly predicted? Table 4.4 lists only those administrations that were in the top 20th (most over-predicted) and bottom 20th (most under-predicted) percentiles. First and foremost, note that most of the incorrect cases are overpredictions, administrations that were at a heightened risk for crisis, but where a crisis did not occur. Among these cases, it is striking that all but one of these (i.e., Menem) represents an unelected replacement administration, whose leaders followed on the heels of previously ousted presidents. In Ecuador following a brief power struggle with then-Vice President

Panama, 7; Paraguay, 6; Peru, 13; Uruguay, 11; and Venezuela, 7. Countries that score 6 or lower on the presidential power scale include the Dominican Republic, 5; El Salvador, 5; Honduras, 3; Mexico, 1; and Nicaragua, 4.

TABLE 4.3: *Predicting Latin American Presidential Crises at the Administration Level from 1985 to 2008 Using the Interactive Model*

	Crisis Observed	No Crisis Observed	
Crisis Predicted	13	6	19 Total predictions of Crises
No Crisis Predicted	19	73	92 Total predictions of No Crises
	32 Crisis Observations	79 No Crisis Observations	

TABLE 4.4: *Examining Over- and Under-predicted Cases*

Administration	Presidential Status	Presidential Power	Crisis Prediction	Appointed
Alarcón	Minority	16	Over	Yes
Duhalde	Minority	8	Over	Yes
Menem, 2nd term	Minority	8	Over	No
Mesa	Minority	8	Over	Yes
Noboa	Minority	16	Over	Yes
Rodríguez	Minority	8	Over	Yes
Samper	Majority	11	Under	No

Rosalía Arteaga, Fabián Alarcón took over after Abdalá Bucaram was ousted in 1997. Three years later, Gustavo Noboa replaced Jamil Mahuad. In Bolivia, Carlos Mesa served as the interim president after Gonzalo Sánchez de Lozada was forced out during his second term in 2003. Eduardo Rodríguez, in turn, then took over from Carlos Mesa in 2005. In Argentina, Eduardo Duhalde, following brief stints by three other politicians, took over from Fernando de la Rúa in 2001. The fact that these replacement presidents managed to survive despite adverse conditions is plausibly due to the fact that these were presidents who were appointed by Congress directly, as in the cases of Alarcón and Duhalde; who had a well-defined short-term mandate, such as Noboa; or who had no political affiliation whatsoever, such as Rodríguez, who was the former Bolivian Supreme Court Chief Justice. These were presidents, in other words, from whom Congress had little to fear.

Turning to the underpredicted case, Samper's administration in Colombia, the president's congressional majority clearly drove down the probability of crisis. Indeed, ultimately this majority was enough to save the president from removal (Pérez-Liñán, 2007), though it was not sufficient to deter the opposition from threatening him with impeachment once allegations broke that drug money had been used to finance the presidential campaign.

4.2.3 Robustness Checks

Thus far, we have shown that the core interactive model outperforms the conventional model of presidential crisis. We have also shown that increasing the president's formal constitutional powers substantially increases the odds of presidential crisis, but only among presidents who lack majority partisan support. In addition, we have established that, overall, the core interactive model does an admirable job in helping us to accurately predict when crises occur and when they do not. In the handful of cases where reality departs from the model's expectations, we have identified plausible reasons that fit with the overall theory. Still, to ensure that that our results are not driven by any of the particular measures we used to capture the main theoretical concepts of interest, this section checks the robustness of our findings using the range of alternative measures described above to estimate the core interactive model.

Robustness Check I: Fixed and Random Effects, and Regime Instability. One possible objection to the results presented thus far hinges on unobserved country or administration characteristics. However, because six of the eighteen Latin American countries (Chile, Costa Rica, Honduras, Mexico, Panama, and Uruguay) did not experience any presidential crises between 1985 to 2008, any model with country-fixed effects ends up dropping a third of all observations (i.e., the core model is reduced from $N = 454$ to $N = 292$). Thus, I instead reran the core interactive model with random effects at both the country level and the administrative level (Model 4.5 in Table 4.5). Although the coefficient for the interaction term falls just shy of statistical significance at the country level, the results are robust at the administration level.

To deal with the lingering concern that presidential crises are still being driven by a country's hidden proclivity toward instability, I also reran the core model with a control for past regime instability. As described above, this measure, *Regime Transitions*, uses the number of regime transitions that occurred in each country between 1950 and 1990 to capture each country's underlying tendency toward instability.

TABLE 4.5: *Robustness Checks I and II*

	(Model 4.5) Random Effects	(Model 4.6) Regime Transition	(Model 4.7) Excludes Marginal Cases	(Model 4.8) Successful Cases
Minority President	-0.84	-0.84	-0.97	-0.77
	(1.03)	(0.97)	(1.04)	(1.01)
Presidential Power	-0.11	-0.11	-0.09	-.17*
	(0.12)	(0.10)	(0.10)	(0.10)
Minority × Power	0.24*	0.24**	0.23**	0.29***
	(0.13)	(0.11)	(0.11)	(0.09)
Protest	0.33***	0.33***	0.27***	0.41***
	0.09	(0.08)	(0.10)	(0.13)
Regime Transitions		0.003		
		(0.12)		
Constant	-1.15	-1.22	-2.98***	-4.08***
	(2.90)	(2.76)	(0.10)	(1.12)
N	454	454	447	431
Wald chi-square	26.31			
Log likelihood	-111.73517			

*$p < 0.1$,
**$p < 0.05$,
***$p < 0.01$.

Importantly, the main results connecting powerful minority presidents to presidential crises do not change. Perhaps more remarkably, there appears to be no relationship between past regime instability and contemporary governmental instability.

Robustness Check II: Restricting the Dependent Variable. Recalling the previous concern that not all legislatures necessarily play an equally important role in every presidential crisis, Model 4.7 allows us to assess whether our results remain similar to the core interactive model if we exclude the six cases in which the legislature played a relatively peripheral role in ousting the president (i.e., Belaguer, 1994; Mahuad, 1999; Fujimori, 2000; de la Rúa, 2001; and Sánchez de Lozada, 2003). Model 4.8, in turn, limits the dependent variable to only those thirteen instances in which presidents were successfully removed by the legislature (i.e., Siles, 1985; Sarney, 1987; Collar, 1992; Pérez, 1992; Serrano, 1993; Belaguer, 1994; Bucaram, 1997; Cubas, 1998; Mahuad, 1999; Fujimori, 2000; de la Rúa, 2001; Sánchez de Lozada, 2003; Gutiérrez, 2005).

In accordance with our theoretical expectations, the interaction terms for both models continue to be significant and positive; indeed, if anything, the conditional effects are slightly enhanced in the second model. Moreover, the coefficients for *Protest* continue to be positive and significant. The only difference is that now the coefficient for *Presidential Power* is statistically significant. However, the fact that there are only two cases in which majority presidents are successfully removed means that we should not make too much of this result.

Robustness Check III: Aggregate versus Component Indices. As discussed above, existing measures of presidential power rely on indices that are constructed through additive aggregation. Recently, however, Olmsted, Signorino and Xiang (2015) have shown analytically that aggregate indices carry the strong assumption that the coefficients for the constituent measures contained in the index are equal. Because this assumption may not be warranted, Olmsted et al. (2015) developed a simple statistical test for disaggregation. Following their protocol, I proceed in three stages. First, I attempt to estimate a fully disaggregated model in which each of the twelve component measures that make up the Alemán and Tsebelis index are included as separate variables and as interaction terms. Hidden collinearity among the independent variables prevents the model from converging, suggesting that a fully disaggregated index is not appropriate in this case. Next, I employ the original theoretical criteria used by Alemán and Tsebelis (2005) to group the twelve constituent variables into four main components: financial legislation, shaping bills, proactive powers, and reactive powers. Interestingly, the conditional relationship uncovered in the original core model appears to be driven entirely by proactive and reactive powers. While the constituent terms are negative and significant, the interaction terms for the presidential powers that determine final passage are both positive and statistically significant at the 0.00 level. To adjudicate between the component-based model and the index-based model I then run a likelihood ratio test following the method outlined in Olmsted et al. (2015). The results, shown in Table 4.6, reveal that the component-based model indeed provides a better fit, which suggests that a theoretically driven disaggregation of presidential power is appropriate.

Robustness Check IV: Alternative Indices of Presidential Power: Models 4.10–4.13 in Table 4.7 explore the consequences of substituting the two alternative measures for institutional powers, *Presidential Power_SM* and *Presidential Power_N*. Recall that *Presidential Power_SM* employs the original fourfold typology of presidential power developed by Mainwaring and Shugart (1997) and focuses entirely on presidents' reactive and

TABLE 4.6: *Robustness Check III*

Variable Name	Core Interactive (Model 4.3)	Components (Model 4.9)
Minority President	−0.84 (0.93)	−26.7*** (5.46)
Power	−0.11 (0.10)	
Minority President × Power	0.24** (0.11)	
Financial Legislation		1.90 (1.17)
Shaping Bills		−1.03 (1.13)
Reactive Power		−10.5*** (2.65)
Proactive Power		−3.75*** (0.87)
Minority × Financial Leg		−0.26 (1.03)
Minority × Shaping Bills		−0.46 (1.33)
Minority × Reactive		10.83*** (2.78)
Minority × Proactive		4.60*** (0.80)
Protest	0.326*** (0.08)	0.39*** (0.11)
Constant	−3.00*** (0.96)	20.0*** (5.10)
N	454	454

$^*p < 0.1$,
$^{**}p < 0.05$,
$^{***}p < 0.01$.

proactive powers.[25] Given the component-based findings, it would be particularly surprising if this robustness check failed. Reassuringly, the coefficients for the core interaction term and for protests remain positive and significant at the 0.05 level.

Presidential Power_N is similar to the original index developed by Alemán and Tsebelis, but also allows us to take constitutional changes in the president's institutional powers into account. Admittedly, the results from this check are less encouraging. Perhaps due to the lower correlation between the original components and Negretto's components, the only term that is significant is *Shaping Bills*, but it is in the wrong direction. To get a better sense of what may be driving these results, I estimate two split models, 4.12 and 4.13.[26] Here, the

[25] Note that Guatemala is not included in the table of presidential powers contained in Mainwaring and Shugart (1997: 49).

[26] The difference between the core interaction model and the two split models is that the interaction model allows us to assess the effects of presidential powers on minority governments compared with their effects on majority governments. By contrast, the split models merely show the effects of presidential powers on each type of government and cannot be directly compared.

TABLE 4.7: *Robustness Check IV*

Variable Name	Shugart and Mainwaring Interactive Model (Model 4.10)	Negretto Interactive Model (Model 4.11)	Negretto Split Model (Minority President = 1) (Model 4.12)	Negretto Split Model (Minority President = 0) (Model 4.13)
Minority President	−1.24 (1.16)	0.55 (2.63)		
Power	−0.55 (0.47)			
Minority President × Power	1.03** (0.49)			
Financial Legislation		−0.80 (1.14)	−0.27 (0.61)	−0.80 (1.03)
Shaping Bills		2.63*** (0.98)	1.04** (0.41)	2.54*** (0.93)
Reactive Power		−2.19 (2.51)	−0.16 (0.63)	−2.24 (2.52)
Proactive Power		0.11 (0.88)	0.79* (0.43)	0.20 (0.85)
Minority × Financial Legislation		0.51 (1.28)		
Minority × Shaping Bills		−1.60 (0.97)		
Minority × Reactive		2.03 (2.46)		
Minority × Proactive		0.70 (0.86)		
Protest	0.32*** (0.08)	0.34*** (0.06)	0.38*** (0.09)	0.23 (0.18)
Constant	−2.53** (1.07)	−4.18 (2.66)	−4.01*** (0.94)	−3.15 (2.61)
N	431	454	279	175

* $p < 0.1$,
** $p < 0.05$,
*** $p < 0.01$.

98

TABLE 4.8: *Robustness Check V*

	Shield (Model 4.14)	Minority Solution (Model 4.15)	Minority Situation Only (Model 4.16)	Non-minority Situation Only (Model 4.17)
Shield	−0.28 (0.80)			
Minority Situation		0.33 (1.30)		
Presidential Power	−0.09 (0.09)	0.02 (0.15)	0.11* (0.06)	0.02 (0.14)
Shield × *Power*	0.20** (0.10)			
Minority Situation × Power		0.09 (0.14)		
Protest	0.34*** (0.08)	0.29*** (0.08)	0.37*** (0.11)	0.12 (0.16)
Constant	−3.24*** (0.08)	−3.71*** (1.26)	−3.40*** (0.66)	−3.29** (1.27)
N	454	301	127	174

* $p < 0.1$,
** $p < 0.05$,
*** $p < 0.01$.

coefficients for *Shaping Bills* are again positive and significant for both models, as is the coefficient for *Proactive Powers* among minority presidents, which is in line with the main result from the component-based model.

Robustness Check V: Alternative Measures of Minority. Next, Models 4.14–4.17 in Table 4.8 assess the impact of altering the measure for partisan powers, substituting *Shield* and *Minority Situation* for *Minority President*. The results in Model 4.14 are fully in line with the core interactive model, whereas the results from Model 4.15 are less supportive. Thus, I again split the sample between administrations with and without minority situations. If the underlying theoretical story is correct, we should see that the coefficients for the president's formal powers and protests are positive and significant in the first sample (Model 4.16), but not in the second (Model 4.17). This is precisely what we find.

Robustness Check VI: Alternative Measures of Cost. Finally, Models 4.18 and 4.19 in Table 4.9 employ alternative measures to capture the legislature's costs for removing the president. In Model 4.18, which uses *Scandals* rather than *Protests*, both of the coefficients for *Scandals* and the

TABLE 4.9: *Robustness Check VI*

	Presidential Scandals (Model 4.18)	Lagged Confidence in President (Model 4.19)
Minority President	−1.59*	−1.84
	(0.96)	(1.49)
Presidential Power	−0.14	−0.20*
	(0.09)	(0.11)
Minority President	0.26***	0.28*
× Power	(0.10)	(0.15)
Scandals	1.40***	
	(0.38)	
Lagged Confidence		−0.01
		(0.01)
Constant	−2.19**	−1.72
	(0.89)	(1.37)
N	372	227

* $p < 0.1$,
** $p < 0.05$,
*** $p < 0.01$.

core interaction term, *Minority Power*, are in the correct direction and statistically significant. Turning to Model 4.19, the fact that the number of observations is cut by more than half due to missing observations means that we cannot put too much stock in these results. Here, the coefficient for *Public Support* is in the right direction, though not statistically significant, while the core interaction term remains positive and significant.[27]

4.3 CONCLUSION

Nearly two decades ago, Mainwaring and Shugart neatly concluded their seminal work on presidential systems in Latin America by suggesting that countries with more extensive powers granted to the executive branch tend to be more crisis ridden (1997, 436). Yet more recently, numerous studies on presidential crises without regime breakdown have either overlooked this key insight or found little systematic support for it. In

---

[27] Note that if we run Model 4.19 with nonlagged confidence scores, we get the same results for the interaction term, but now the coefficient for confidence is negative and significant, suggesting that presidential crises may also lower the executive's popularity. I explore this endogeneity more fully in Chapter 7.

this chapter, by contrast, I have explored the alternative claim derived from the bargaining model presented in the previous chapter that the president's formal powers do indeed matter, but only under certain circumstances.

Drawing on the relevant data from the ICLA dataset, this chapter has provided systematic empirical evidence consistent with my overarching expectation that having greater formal powers tends to put the president at a greater risk of crisis, but only if the president also lacks sufficient partisan support. Specifically, I have shown that compared with existing multivariate models, the interactive model predicted by my theoretical framework not only performs as predicted, but also fits the empirical data better than its competitors. In addition to exploring the substantive effects of this interaction on the likelihood of presidential crises, I then briefly discussed how the cases that are incorrectly predicted by the statistical model are nevertheless roughly consistent with the book's general theoretical framework. Last but not least, I sought to further verify the robustness of the interaction effect between presidential de facto and de jure powers by subjecting my initial results to multiple specifications of the estimation strategy and to different measures for each of the three main component variables. Having plumbed the quantitative evidence on presidential crises, the next two chapters explore how far the inter-branch bargaining framework takes us in explaining the onset of other types of institutional crises.

5

Constitutional Coups as a Commitment Problem

Correa wins, but how long will he last?
— Andean Group, December 2006

Whereas most Latin America experts assume that constitutional coups constitute prima facie evidence that presidents are omnipotent, the main implication of the dynamic version of the bargaining model presented in Chapter 3 is that leaders target legislatures precisely because they are not. Rather, my argument is that such crises are roughly analogous to offensive strikes; presidents launch them in anticipation of having their own political life spans cut short by congressional opposition. Of course, it is worth highlighting at the outset that legislative crises are both relatively difficult and costly to carry out under democracy. Unlike presidential ousters, which were the focus of the previous chapter, or judicial manipulation, which is the subject of the next chapter, there are no clear constitutional procedures – save revising the constitution itself – that legally enable presidents to remove and remake Congress. This alone arguably explains the global fact that legislative crises are comparatively much rarer than either presidential or judicial crises.

According to the theory laid out in Chapter 3, constitutional coups – when they do occur – are driven by an underlying commitment problem rooted in the gap between the presidents' de jure powers and de facto powers. Once this gap emerges, we have seen that the legislative opposition cannot credibly promise to allow the president to complete his or her term in office. As such, presidents who have good reason to suspect that conditions will shift against them face an incentive to launch an offensive strike against the legislature. Deploying a combination of quantitative and qualitative evidence, the rest of the chapter sets out to evaluate my argument. While rejecting any single null hypothesis associated with the core mechanism cannot definitely supply an answer, taken together the general pattern of evidence uncovered in this chapter is wholly consistent with the dynamic bargaining account.

5.1 STATISTICAL EVIDENCE

To begin to assess whether presidents target legislatures preventively, this section draws on the subset of the ICLA dataset, which includes a complete sample – both legislative crises and noncrises – involving the executive-legislative ordered dyad. Starting with a discussion of whether the same threshold crisis conditions that put presidents at risk for early removal also help us to predict the onset of legislative crises, I compare the statistical evidence for this hypothesis with an alternative scenario in which institutionally weak minority presidents exploit their popularity to stage legislative crises and expand power. I then consider whether past experiences of presidential crises and/or a history of the conditions that produce them (i.e., previous presidents have tended to lose seat shares in midterm elections, or popularity over time) increase the likelihood of legislative crises relative to noncrises. The third section considers whether public support for the legislature and older parties constrains presidents from launching legislative coups. Finally, the fourth section tests the intuitively appealing proposition that if legislative crises are broadly preventive, they should be clustered relatively early in a president's term. Given the low ratio of legislative crises to noncrises (in this case, inter-branch crises constitute 9 of 474, or just 0.02 percent of the data), I again employ rare events logistic regression throughout to estimate each of the statistical models, and, as in the previous chapter, I cluster the standard errors by country.

5.1.1 Threshold Crisis Conditions

Recalling the dynamic bargaining model analyzed in Chapter 3, I hypothesized that the same core conditions that put presidents at risk (i.e., $p - d > q$) should increase the probability of a legislative crisis as well. The reason is that shifting q to the left makes it that much easier for legislatures to reach the threshold that incentivizes them to launch a presidential attack. In other words, the more constitutional power the president has to begin with, the less the other conditions, such as losing partisan support or popularity, need to shift against him or her for the legislature's commitment problem to emerge. Thus, the first testable implication is that, conditional on the president being in the minority, the probability of a legislative crisis increases in the amount of constitutional power allocated to the president.

However, notice that the payoffs to the executive for launching a legislative strike ($E^* = d - c$)[1] also potentially admit an alternative mechanism in which legislative crises are driven instead by the gap between the president's popularity and his or her lack of de jure powers. To give one example, when Hugo Chávez convened the constituent assembly, his enormous popular support arguably far outstripped his initial partisan support and constitutional powers; perhaps he was simply trying to exploit his popularity rather than slay the specter of removal.[2] While in any real-world example both motivations may coexist, the question taken up here is which motivation systematically increases the likelihood of legislative crises. If the latter, then the likelihood of legislative crises should increase with presidential popularity among minority presidents, particularly at low levels of constitutional power. If the former, then legislative crises should increase with constitutional power, conditional on the president being in the minority.

To adjudicate between these different possibilities, I estimate two models (5.1 and 5.2) in Table 5.1. The first replicates the core model from the previous chapter, but regresses the president's partisan status, his constitutional powers, and their interaction on legislative crises. For the sake of consistency with the core model from the previous chapter, I also include the term *Protest* in Model 5.1. Interestingly, because this measure includes all antigovernmental protests, it potentially encompasses protests against both branches of government. To the extent that the protests are aimed at the executive, the coefficient can be interpreted, as in Chapter 4, as capturing the cost to the legislature for attacking the president. To the extent that the protests are aimed at Congress, however, the coefficient might be interpreted as the cost to the president for attacking the legislature. In any event, we would expect a positive effect on legislative crises, driven either by an elevated risk to the president or by a reduced cost to the president. The second model regresses the president's popularity,

---

[1] Recall from Chapter 3 that the executive's payoffs for staging a legislative crisis simplify to $d - c = E^*$, where capturing the pie effectively means moving q (and p) all the way to the left and minimizing the legislature's payoff (and opposition seat share) to 0.

[2] Despite high abstention rates, Chávez garnered more support in the presidential election than any other candidate had since Romulo Gallegos in 1947 (Coppedge 2003).

TABLE 5.1: *Legislative Crises and Threshold Effects*

Variable	Model 5.1	Model 5.2
Minority President	−2.33	
	(1.77)	
Presidential Powers	−0.45***	0.73***
	(0.15)	(0.17)
Minority President × Power	0.59***	
	(0.16)	
Protest	0.31*	
	(0.17)	
Presidential Popularity		−0.05***
		(0.01)
Presidential Popularity × Presidential Powers		0.004***
		(0.001)
Constant	−3.09**	−12.59***
	(1.34)	(2.67)
N	454	157

* $p < 0.1$,
** $p < 0.05$,
*** $p < 0.01$.

constitutional powers, and their interaction on legislative crises among minority presidents. If such presidents are indeed seeking to exploit their popularity, then we would expect a positive coefficient for the constituent term, *Presidential Popularity,* which effectively captures the impact of popularity on constitutional coups when presidential power is at its weakest.

Fully in line with the first hypothesis, the coefficient for the interaction term contained in Model 5.1 reveals that the probability of a legislative crisis significantly increases, the more constitutional power the president has, contingent on him or her being in the minority. The coefficient for *Protest* is also positive and significant, as expected. As in Chapter 4, the marginal effect of being in the minority, as shown in Figure 5.1, achieves significance once presidents have reached a certain threshold of constitutional powers (roughly 7 of 16).

Conversely, the results contained in Model 5.2 are exactly the opposite of what the popularity hypothesis suggests. Although restricting the sample to minority presidents and the lack of public opinion data reduces the number of observations dramatically,[3] we see very little support for the

---

[3] As in Chapter 4, popularity scores for each observation are generated by multiplying the percentage of respondents in each category reporting confidence in the executive and then

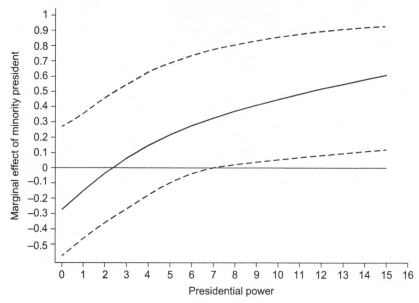

FIGURE 5.1: Marginal effects of presidential power on legislative crises among minority presidents.

notion that the likelihood of legislative coups among weaker presidents increases with presidential popularity. That the coefficient for presidential popularity is negative and significant further reveals that popularity instead drives down the likelihood of a constitutional coup, thus suggesting that – Chávez aside – public support may help substitute for a lack of constitutional power, rather than trigger a grab for it.[4]

5.1.2 Past Vulnerability as Future Risk

Intuitively, we might imagine that the vulnerability of previous presidents also influences leaders' beliefs about the probability that the legislature will succeed in ousting them. In addition to exploring the effects of the current political environment on constitutional coups, I thus hypothesized that the

adding them together as follows: "a lot" × 2 + "some" × 1 + "a little" × – 1 + "none" × – 2. Although this specification clearly introduces the problem of endogeneity, the variable is not lagged because most attacks occur early in the president's term and I want to capture the current president's popularity, not his predecessor's.

[4] Indeed, if we simply compare the means of presidential popularity among presidents who target legislatures with those who do not, the former is roughly 20 points lower than latter.

TABLE 5.2: *Legislative Crises and Past Presidential Vulnerability*

Variable	Model 5.3	Model 5.4	Model 5.5
Presidential Powers		0.01	0.27*
		(0.10)	(0.15)
Protest		0.28*	
		(0.16)	
Predecessors	0.37***		
	(0.07)		
Past Seat Loss		−3.03	
		(2.12)	
Past Seat Loss × Power		0.25*	
		(0.15)	
Past Popularity_Gain			−0.02**
			(0.01)
Constant	−4.55***	−4.33***	−7.19***
	(0.50)	(1.03)	(1.87)
N	474	454	105

* $p < 0.1$,
** $p < 0.05$,
*** $p < 0.01$.

incumbent's decision might also be influenced by the past experiences of presidents in their countries. Specifically, I argue that the risk for constitutional coups should be elevated where the president's predecessors have been challenged and/or in contexts where the incumbent's predecessor has rapidly lost popular or partisan support. The actions taken by Chávez and Correa described below hint at just this sort of reasoning: previous leaders in their countries had been marginalized and then forced from power at the hands of the opposition; why wait and suffer the same fate?

To explore whether past vulnerability can help account systematically for the onset of legislative crises, I estimate three separate models, shown in Table 5.2. In the first (Model 5.3), I construct *Predecessors*, which represents the number of previous administrations in a given country that suffered a presidential crisis.[5] In the next model, I construct *Past Seat Loss*, which calculates the percentage of lower house seats lost or gained

---

[5] Given that constructing the variable in this way adds a temporal component, I also run the model using a dummy variable, which simply records whether the previous government suffered a presidential crisis or not. In addition, given the number of presidential crises that occurred in Ecuador, I also ran the model excluding Ecuador. The results remain robust for both alternative specifications.

by the president's party for each previous administration, and create an annual rolling sum of the average previous changes for each administration.[6] To the extent that this measure represents a prospective measure of p in the original model, I then recode it as a dummy variable and interact it with *Power* to examine whether institutionally strong leaders who operate in electorally volatile environments are more likely to preemptively act against the legislature than leaders who do not. The third model (5.5), in turn, relates to d, or the president's popularity. In contexts where public support has been fickle, presidents may well fear that their support is also likely to evaporate over time, thus making it that much easier for the opposition to oust them. To capture this, the measure *Past Popularity_Gain* is constructed by calculating the difference in the previous administration's popularity at the beginning and at the end of its term.[7]

The results contained in Table 5.2 support each of the three testable implications connected to the dynamic bargaining theory. Translating the results of the first univariate model (5.3), Figure 5.2 shows that the predicted probability of a legislative crisis increases from less than 1 percent under administrations without a history of attacks to almost 30 percent among administrations with multiple previous attacks.

Turning to Model 5.4, the coefficient for the interaction term, *Past Seat Loss* × *Power*, is also precisely what we would expect if presidents are using information about electoral volatility to estimate their chances of risk. The predicted probabilities displayed in Figure 5.3 show that the probability of a legislative crisis increases again with presidential power, but only for those leaders operating in contexts where their predecessors have lost seats.

Turning to Model 5.5, here I am exploring whether presidents are influenced by their predecessors' loss of public support. Again, given the limited number of observations due to the lack of public opinion data, it is hard to put too much weight on the results contained in Model 5.5. Indeed, the core conditional model cannot be fully estimated because all of the presidents left in the sample that launch legislative crises are in the minority. Rather, we

---

[6] Note that the dummy variable *Past Seat Loss* has more 0s than 1s, although the differences in no seat loss or seat gain are smaller than the differences in losses. On average, Latin American administrations tend to lose seats over time by roughly 3.7 percent.

[7] On average, Latin American presidents are not popular. The mean score for confidence in the executive is −43.8. If we look at the evolution of public support over time, presidents tend to lose support over their terms. Excluding the Kirchner administration (2003–2007), which was an extreme outlier, the variable *Past Popularity_Gain* ranges from −92 to 148 and the mean is −6.15.

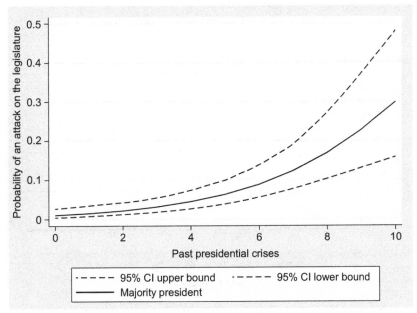

FIGURE 5.2: Predicted probability of legislative crises by past presidential crises.

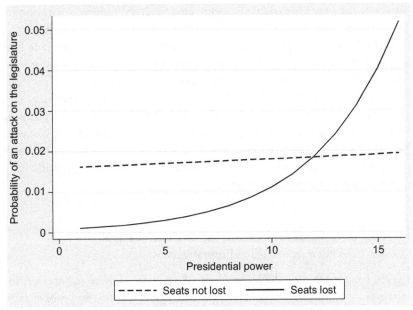

FIGURE 5.3: Predicted probability of legislative crises by past presidential seat loss.

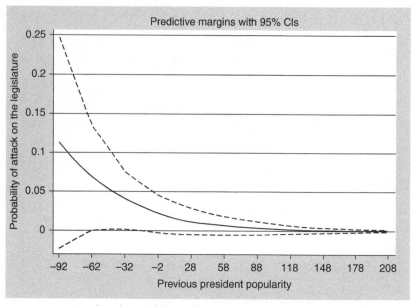

FIGURE 5.4: Predicted probability of legislative crises by past presidential popularity swing.

can consider only the variable *Power* to effectively gauge how constitutional powers affect legislative crises among this subset. Importantly, however, even in this reduced sample, both of the coefficients for *Power* and for *Past Popularity_Gain* are significant and in the right direction. As Figure 5.4 shows, however, the effects are largely confined to cases in which previous presidents have lost popularity, but the low number of observations prevents us from having too much faith in these results. Having a predecessor who suffered the largest decline in popularity (−92) compared with one who did not lose any public support over the course of his or her term increases the probability of a legislative crisis under the successor government by approximately 10 percentage points.

5.1.3 Costs to the President: Legislative Popularity and Traditional Parties

Next, I consider two different types of costs presidents might face for attempting legislative coups. As shown in Table 5.3, the first model (5.6) approximates the price of breaking the institutional order by using the public's confidence in the legislature. Similar to the measures for presidential

TABLE 5.3: *Legislative Crises, Costs to the President, and Timing*

Variable	Model 5.6	Model 5.7	Model 5.8	Model 5.9
Minority President				−2.20
				(1.45)
Presidential Powers	0.09			−0.68***
	(0.07)			(0.20)
Minority President ×				0.65***
Presidential Powers				(0.18)
Legislature's Popularity	−0.03			
(lag)	(0.02)			
Predecessors				0.37*
				(0.21)
Past Seat Loss				−1.94*
				(1.16)
Party Age		−0.72***		−0.67*
		(0.25)		(0.35)
Term Year			−0.62***	−0.45***
			(0.23)	(0.17)
Constant	−7.6***	−2.00***	−2.45***	1.54
	(2.64)	(0.45)	(0.57)	(1.38)
N	227	474	474	474

* $p < 0.1$,
** $p < 0.05$,
*** $p < 0.01$.

support, I construct a legislative confidence score by drawing on public opinion results from the Latinobarómetro surveys and lagging the score by one year. The expectation is simply that the more public confidence that the legislature enjoys, the less likely presidents are to launch an attack. The results contained in Model 5.6 again must be interpreted with some caution due to the low number of observations, but they certainly suggest that, all else equal, the less popular the legislature is, the more likely presidents are to attack it. The coefficient is negative, as expected, and, with the p-value 0.108, falls just shy of statistical significance.

The second model (5.7) explores how the potential cost for the president might be influenced by his or her party. Indeed, as we shall see below, leaders who gained notoriety for attacking their legislatures have tended to be political outsiders, associated with relatively young and inchoate political parties or movements. Following the implosion of the traditional party systems in Peru and Venezuela, both Fujimori and Chávez forged plebiscitarian democracies that largely eschewed institutionalization (Levitsky and Cameron, 2003;

Tanaka, 2005). In Ecuador, Correa has followed a similar trajectory, emphatically rejecting traditional political parties and governing instead via a "permanent campaign," which aims to appeal directly to the public (Conaghan, 2008).

Here I use age as a proxy for party strength (cf. Stokes, 2001) to explore whether it is more costly for presidents who belong to established parties to disrupt the institutional order by staging a legislative attack. The empirical question taken up here is two-fold. First, beyond these signal cases, is party age negatively correlated with the onset of legislative crisis? And, second, is this consistent with the logic that older parties actually raise the costs of an attack for presidents, or simply because presidents from younger parties also tend to control fewer seats in the legislature? In other words, are older parties effectively constraining presidents, or just making it more likely that the two branches are compatible?

According to the result of Model 5.7, younger parties indeed raise the probability of legislative crises.[8] In purely descriptive terms, among the full set of presidents who threatened or launched legislative crises, the mean age of presidential parties was just twenty-six years. Among the null cases, by contrast, the average age for the leaders' parties nearly doubles, to fifty-five years. Figure 5.5 shows the predicted probabilities dropping from around 12 percent among the youngest parties to less than 1 percent among the oldest parties.

To adjudicate between the two foregoing interpretations (parties as constraints versus parties as proxies for minority status) I also ran two separate models (not shown here) that control for the percentage of seats held by the president's party and minority status, respectively. The results suggest that presidents are indeed independently constrained by older parties regardless of the number of seats they control, thus lending further support to the hypothesis that parties constrain leaders.

5.1.4 Timing

Finally, to what extent does timing affect the odds of a legislative crisis? The basic intuition is that if such crises are preventive, then, ipso facto, they should occur relatively early in a president's term. This is so for at least two reasons. First, at a certain point, there is simply no more shadow of the future

---

[8] *Party Age* is the logged measure of the number of years that the president's party has been in existence.

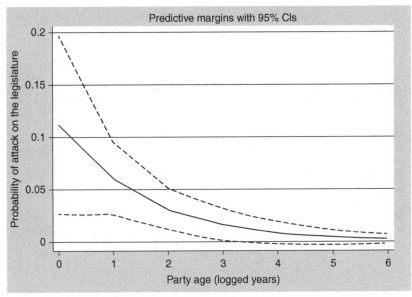

FIGURE 5.5: Predicted probability of legislative crises by party age.

to confront. Hence, the value of a preventive strike arguably declines as the end of a president's term in office draws near. Second, to the extent that some of the factors that we have already identified as contributing to the president's strategic advantage tend to have a temporal component (i.e., seat share modestly declines over the course of their administration; see note 10), it makes good sense for the president to capitalize on his de facto power before the tide shifts. To see whether timing matters in practice, here I construct the variable *Term Year*, which records how many years the current administration has been in office. In line with our expectations, the results contained in Model 5.8 and graphed in Figure 5.6 show that the odds of a legislative crisis do decline, albeit rather modestly, after the two years of the president's administration, falling monotonically from a high of 3.5 percent in the first year, to less than 1 percent in the fourth year.

5.1.5 Putting It All Together

The statistical results largely remain intact when we combine the variables into a single multivariate model. Specifically, as Model 5.9 shows, the interaction effect connected with the core crisis threshold hypothesis persists.

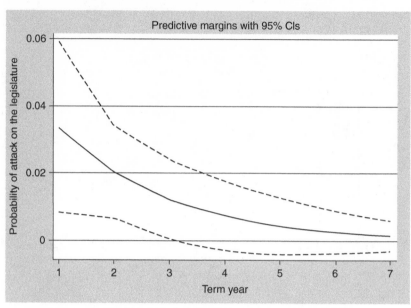

FIGURE 5.6: Predicted probability of legislative crises by term year.

Presidents who are themselves currently at risk of an attack continue to be more likely than their more stable counterparts to stage an attack against the legislature. Conversely, presidents who enjoy both strong institutional powers and strong partisan powers (as shown by the negative coefficient for *Presidential Power*) have little need for such tactics. Moreover, the negative coefficient for *Minority President* continues to support the rather counterintuitive claim that simply being in the minority is not a sufficient trigger. Rather, precisely because institutionally weak minority presidents are at less risk of an attack themselves, these leaders are also less likely to go after their legislatures. Likewise, the coefficients for *Party Age* and *Term Year* also remain significant and are in the expected direction. Note that the coefficient for *Predecessors* now loses significance, but if we run the full model with the alternative specification (with *Predecessors* as a dummy variable instead of a count variable), then the significance returns.[9]

---

[9] Of course, if legislative crises are rooted in the desire to avert presidential crises, then this begs the question of why more than three-quarters of administrations that ultimately endured presidential crises failed to act preventively. In other words, why didn't all presidents under threat of removal at least attempt to wage an offensive counterattack? Beyond the broader points made at the outset of this chapter regarding the legal barriers

Indeed, the only variable that does not behave as expected in the multivariate model is the coefficient for *Past Seat Loss*, which is significant, but now is in the opposite direction. In other words, once we control for all risk factors together, it seems that the experience of previous presidents losing seats actually decreases the chances of a legislative crisis. Of course, it is important to recall that in the earlier version of Model 5.3, *Past Seat Loss* was itself interacted with *Power*. Thus, including *Past Seat Loss* as a separate variable essentially measures its impact when *Power* is held constant and, therefore, does not adequately capture the original interaction that the underlying bargaining story implies. In fact, if we run the multivariate model (not shown here) and instead substitute an interaction between *Past Seat Loss* and *Power*, the rest of the results remain the same but now the positive effect of *Past Seat Loss* conditional on presidential powers returns, though the coefficient capturing the conditional relationship is no longer significant.

5.2 CASE STUDIES

Having pushed the quantitative evidence as far as it will allow, the second half of the chapter focuses on four of the region's most notorious legislative crises. For if the mechanism of survival is not operative in these signal cases, then the theory is of little use for understanding how events unfolded on the ground. Starting with an examination of the *autogolpe* (self-coup) carried out in 1992 by Alberto Fujimori in Peru, I trace the failed Guatemalan *autogolpe* staged by Jorge Elias Serrano the following year, as well as chart the more recent efforts of Hugo Chávez in Venezuela and Rafael Correa in Ecuador to dissolve their legislatures by convoking constituent assemblies. Drawing on a range of evidence from newspaper accounts and secondary sources, as well as a series of interviews that I conducted with more than twenty political elites in Ecuador during July

presidents face to carrying out a legislative attack, the bargaining logic suggests that the same risk factors that distinguish legislative crises from all null cases ($n = 474$) might also help us explain variation within this subset of cases. Given the low number of observations in the presidential crises sample ($n = 36$), here I simply compare the means for the key risk variables identified in the foregoing analysis. In line with the theory, the mean values for *Power* and *Predecessors* were indeed higher among presidents under attack who launched legislative crises compared with those who did not, while the mean values for *Past Popularity_Gain* and *Party Age* were lower. Thus, it appears that in the cases where presidential instability cascaded onto the legislature, presidents had more reasons initially to suspect that they would face such instability.

2008, I build the narrative around exploring whether these leaders had compelling reasons to believe that their own political futures were at stake, and, crucially, whether they could have reasonably thought that capturing the legislature was essential for their own political survival.

5.2.1 Fujimori

Even before Alberto Fujimori took office, the threat of removal loomed over his presidency. Given the disastrous policies of Alan García's previous government, in 1989 the military developed the so-called Plan Verde (Green Plan), in which officers plotted to stage a coup in the event that the right-wing presidential candidate, Mario Vargas Llosa, lost to the left in the 1990 elections (Cameron, 1998; Rospigliosi, 2000; Kenney, 2004). Fujimori's sudden surge of support in the final months of the campaign and his surprising landslide victory over Vargas Llosa did little to assuage the military's abiding concern that the country was slipping further into economic and social chaos. As the military leaderships in charge of the plot warned, "we cannot expect anything certain from Change '90, and the Homeland cannot take any more economic experiments ..." (*Oiga*, July 12, 1993, p. 22, cited in Kenny, 2004: 109). Before his inauguration, Fujimori learned of the pending coup from Vladimir Montesinos, the man who would serve as Fujimori's head of the National Intelligence Service (SIN) during Fujimori's decade in power, and who would later be at the center of the corruption scandal that ultimately led to Fujimori's resignation in 2000 (Cameron, 1998; Kenny, 2004). In response, Fujimori's first act in office was to force several commanding officers into retirement and to name loyal officers to key cabinet positions shortly thereafter (Kenny, 2004: 115).

Although Fujimori managed to effectively thwart the military's attempts to end his presidency before his term began, soon thereafter the president faced an increasingly recalcitrant Congress. For, unlike his two predecessors, Fujimori controlled nowhere near a majority of seats in Congress. Given the organizational weakness of his party, Change '90 had garnered only 23 percent of seats in the upper house and just 18 percent of seats in the lower house. Initially, there seemed to be multiple opportunities for coalition building across the fragmented political spectrum. On the left, the Alianza Popular Revolucionaria Americana (APRA) was willing to back Fujimori provided that he lend his support to former president Alan Garcia, who was facing an ex post impeachment trial on corruption. On the right, the president's sudden turn to neoliberalism was obviously attractive to the various Frente Democrático parties (also known as FREDEMO). Indeed, during his first few months in office Fujimori was able to convince Congress to delegate emergency powers to his administration, allowing him to virtually govern by decree (Schmidt, 1998). Yet just a little more than six months into his term, Fujimori broke with Congress over a harrowing budget dispute, prompting the weekly magazine, *Caretas*, to put Fujimori on its cover with the caption, "In the Crosshairs: Could Fujimori Be Deposed?" (cited in Kenney, 2004: 146).

By November 1991, in the wake of a new series of highly contested economic and national security presidential decrees, the opposition parties in Congress began to study openly the possibility of declaring the president "morally incapacitated." According to the 1979 Constitution, Congress could effectively declare the presidency vacated by this criterion with only a simple majority of votes in both chambers (Kenney, 2004: 183). Although the motion did not pass, the legislative opposition considered the president duly warned. Playing the racial card, one senator remarked that "Fujimori would have to be made to understand by means of 'slaps, kicks, and insults, because that is his origin'" (ibid.: 185).

Following the subsequent passage of a sweeping law to curtail presidential powers coupled with various efforts to repeal Fujimori's decrees, Congress also opened an investigation of first lady Susana Higuchi de Fujimori on corruption charges associated with selling clothing donated from Japan. Although estranged from her husband, such an investigation would have potentially put Fujimori's notoriously secretive inner circle in the spotlight (Schmidt, 1998: 113). As one senior government official remarked of Peruvian politics at the time, "Either Congress would kill the president, or the president would kill the Congress" (cited in Kenney, 2004: 209). Three days later, Fujimori called out the tanks, and the legislature, along with the courts, was effectively dissolved.

5.2.2 Serrano

One year later, a broadly similar inter-branch dynamic unfolded in Guatemala, but yielded a very different outcome. Like Fujimori, Jorge Serrano Elías was a member of his country's growing evangelical minority and an unknown political candidate (Cameron, 1998). Campaigning on the rather vague, if contradictory, platform of law and order and human rights (Stokes 2001; also see *Latin American Weekly Reports*, January 17, 1991), Serrano handily won the 1990 run-off election. His nascent party, Movimiento de Acción Solidaria (MAS), however, failed to capture more than a handful of legislative seats (thirteen of 111). In a move similar to Fujimori's, Serrano initially sought to achieve governability by stacking his cabinet with members of the main opposition parties and the business sector, thus quickly alienating his own supporters.[10]

During his first year in office, Serrano worked hard to secure a peace accord between the military and the guerrillas of the Unidad Revolucionaria Nacional Guatemalteca (URNG). Despite some initial headway, however, in 1992 the parties hit a stalemate. In this context, renewed allegations of military abuse of human rights emerged, prompting the well-known left-wing leader Rigoberta Menchu to remark publicly that a coup against the government was feasible. Though Serrano moved quickly to squelch the rumors, the Human Rights Procurator, Ramiro de León Carpio (the man who would ultimately take over after Serrano was forced into exile in Panama), claimed enigmatically that

... there is ill-will towards politicians generally. In the streets, people are talking about the "tramping of heavy feet" ... What happened in Venezuela and Peru could be applauded in Guatemala.[11]

By the fall, stories in the local press broke about Serrano's alleged plans to imitate Fujimori. At the time, the government refuted the charges by arguing, rather oddly, that the rumors were false because Serrano had already been talked out of emulating his Peruvian counterpart three months earlier.[12] The following spring, however, as Serrano's resumed peace negotiations triggered a series of bombings in Guatemala City, Congress explicitly warned Serrano against traveling abroad, alluding to the fact that leaving the country would potentially open him to "attacks from nationalists, particularly those in the armed forces."[13]

Meanwhile, the very methods that Serrano had deployed in order to secure support from Congress and the courts began to haunt him. Emerging evidence revealed the widespread practice of illegal payoffs arranged by the president to attract support from the opposition (Villagrán de León, 1993). As the facts began to come to light, the opposition started to build a case for dislodging the president from power (Cameron, 1998; Kenney, 2004). It was in the midst of these emerging

---

[10] *LAWR*, January 24, 1991.   [11] *LAWR*, June 4, 1992.

[12] The triggering event supposedly was a decision by Congress to grant immunity to an opposition congressman for releasing his brother, who was being held on drug charges (cited in *LAWR*, October 1, 1992).

[13] *LAWR*, March 25, 1993.

allegations of corruption that Serrano made the fateful decision to stage a self-coup, calling out the army and closing both Congress and the Supreme Court on May 25. As the *Latin American Weekly Report* summarized, "Serrano had acted to pre-empt the presentation to Congress of the petition bearing 5,000 signatures, for the president's impeachment on several charges of corruption."[14]

With civil society united against him and U.S. aid suspended, the army quickly switched sides, and Serrano was forced into exile a week later. Observing his failure, critics have rightly asserted that Serrano, in his haste, made fundamental miscalculations about the domestic and international reaction (Villagrán de León, 1993: 119). In terms of the theory, however, the miscalculation arguably lay not in staging the *autogolpe* but in failing to stage it sooner. In this case, the *autogolpe* was more of a Hail Mary pass as opposed to a well-conceived preventive strike. Serrano's saga thus underscores the fact that sometimes shifts in power may be so rapid that effective preventive strategies are not possible.

5.2.3 Chávez

Hugo Chávez's radical social project deeply threatened the survival of Venezuela's political and economic elite. As such, it is plausible not only that traditional elites were predisposed to remove him from power if and when the opportunity arose, but that Chávez was well aware of the potential threat they posed. Of course, as numerous observers have also remarked, Chávez engaged in a profoundly confrontational leadership style from the very beginning of his presidency (Garcia-Serra 2001; Coppedge 2003). That he held a kind of siege mentality comes across in his frequent reliance on a vocabulary of war. During his first year in office he frequently cited *El Oráculo del Guerrero* (The Oracle of the Warrior). Pondering why this book held such appeal to Chávez, the Argentine author Lucas Estrella put it this way:

I suppose he feels that the only way he will be able to carry out a massive undertaking that lies before him is by following the principles of warrior. [One of these principles, for example, says], "Warrior, when you win a battle don't lose time sheathing your sword, because tomorrow will only bring more battles."

(cited in Marcano and Tyszka, 2007: 138)

[14] *LAWR*, n.d.

Indeed, although the opposition's desire to oust Chávez became only more vehement over time – witness the botched coup attempt in 2002, the mass strike in 2003, and the failed recall referendum in 2004 – there were plenty of signs that his presidency was intolerable to his opponents at the outset. Commenting on his campaign, McCoy writes, "Chávez's dramatic rise made many people nervous. Rumors of assassination plots against the candidate and of a preemptive coup to forestall a Chávez victory abounded" (1999: 67). Another early indication of the depth of the traditional political elites' opposition to Chávez occurred during his inauguration. Breaking a forty-year tradition, outgoing president Rafael Caldera refused to swear in the new president. Remarking on this, Caldera explained, "Without a doubt, I had no desire to confer that sash on Chávez, because I could already sense all the negative aspects of his presidency" (cited in Marcano and Tyszka, 2007: 124).[15]

With the opposition still reeling from its electoral drubbing and Chávez's own popular approval ratings standing at over 90 percent, why wait for circumstances to shift against him? After all, Chávez had started his own political career attempting to remove a sitting president (Carlos Andrés Pérez) who had sought change and was subsequently impeached. Since then, the country had become only more socially and politically polarized along class lines (Coppedge, 2003; Ellner, 2003). And as the election campaign had demonstrated, Chávez clearly faced a political opposition that could put aside its differences to attempt to defeat him. Given that he lacked control over a sufficient number of seats to block an impeachment trial, the opposition could have easily united against him not merely to block his policies (which they had already begun to do), but also to remove him from power.[16] Chávez's dare to Congress to impeach him less than 100 days into his term hints at his

---

[15] According to Caldera, however, there was some precedent for this: in 1969 outgoing president Raúl Leoni had refused to give Caldera the sash (cited in Marcano and Tyszka, 2007: 124).

[16] Like Fujimori and Serrano, Chávez fell well short of obtaining a legislative majority in 1999. Part of this failure, no doubt, was due to recent changes in the electoral laws, which called for nonconcurrent legislative and presidential elections, in that order. At the time, both of the leading candidates accused the outgoing elite of separating the elections as part of a ploy to damage independent candidates (McCoy, 1999: 68). Chávez's party, the Movimiento V República (MVR), came in second to Acción Democrática (AD), winning only about 25 percent of the legislative seats in the November 1990 elections. Together with his electoral coalition, the Polo Patriótico, ultimately he controlled only slightly more than one-third of the seats in the Chamber of Deputies (ibid., 69).

recognition of this potential.[17] Meanwhile, it bears mentioning that finding the legal grounds to do so might not have been all that difficult. According to one of his closest advisors, within the first year alone there were at least forty instances of corruption about which Chávez knew and did nothing (Marcano and Tyszka, 2007: 138). As his predecessor Carlos Andrés Pérez had found out, such cases presumably could easily have been exposed and exploited by the opposition, particularly if the honeymoon period ended and Chávez's popularity began to wane.

5.2.4 Correa

By 2006 Ecuador had become the poster child of institutional instability in the region. Since Sixto Durán-Ballen's administration (1992–1996), not a single elected president had been able to complete his term in office. As the previous chapter recounted, in 1997 Congress ousted Abdalá Bucaram on grounds of mental incapacity. Three years later in the midst of mass protests, Congress removed his successor, Jamil Mahuad, on the trumped-up charges that he had abandoned his post.[18] Lucio Gutiérrez's government, which had attempted to cut a deal with the Partido Roldosista Ecuatoriano (PRE) to remain in power by carrying out one of the most egregious court-packing schemes in Latin American history, became the country's next casualty in April 2005.

In the midst of this enormous political turmoil, Rafael Correa, a young, leftist, U.S.-trained economist, first made a name for himself by joining the Forajido (outlaw) protest movement demanding Gutiérrez's resignation. Appointed subsequently as minister of the economy by Gutiérrez's vice president and successor, Alfredo Palacios, Correa launched his bid for the presidency later that same year, drawing on support from the left and the Forajido movement (Conaghan, 2008: 49). Deeply opposed to the social and economic policies that had been adopted by his country's leaders since the 1990s, Correa pitched himself as a political outsider. Garnering just 23 percent of the vote in the first round, Correa came in second against the three-time presidential candidate and banana magnate,

---

[17] Following the legislature's vain attempts to amend the "Enabling Law," which would have given him vast decree powers over the economy, Chávez publicly warned, "Congress, if it so wishes can impeach me, but I will not turn back ... We'll see who wins this battle. There is no turning back." *LAWR*, July 6, 1999.

[18] According to former President Borja, however, Mahuad went to the airport with the intention of fleeing the country. When he was unable to do so, he ended up in the Chilean Embassy (author interview, July 30, 2008).

Alvaro Noboa, in the first round on October 15, 2006. In the run-off elections held six weeks later, Correa swept to power with 57 percent of the vote. The headline of the *Andean Group Report*, which is quoted at the beginning of this chapter, simply read: "Correa wins, but how long will he last?"

For Correa had made the highly unusual decision not to allow any members of his political movement, the Movimiento Patria Altiva y Soberana (MPAIS), to stand for office in the legislative elections. Given the fragmentation of the party system and the challenge of registering candidates from his nascent party, Correa undoubtedly realized that he could not have won a majority of seats in Congress. Rather than try to rely on his predecessors' obviously failed strategy of "rolling majorities," or makeshift temporary alliances with the traditional parties (Pachano, 2007: 3), Correa's gambit was to undermine the legitimacy of Congress before it could undermine his. "With this one bold stroke," Catherine Conaghan writes, "Correa both unequivocally identified his candidacy with the voters' deeply anti-political mood and accepted the risk that, if elected, he would assume office with zero assurance of legislative support and far greater assurance that legislators might move to oust him at any time" (2008: 50).

Correa's epic battles with Congress over the constituent assembly would dominate the first year of his presidency. Much like Chávez, Correa's initial reassurances that the constituent assembly would not seek to dissolve Congress fell on deaf ears.[19] Indeed, just as in Venezuela, the opposition immediately signaled its deep distrust of Correa by breaking with tradition at his inaugural ceremony, refusing in this case to have the head of the legislature confer the presidential sash on Correa.[20] Immediately after Correa took office, the opposition parties formed an "anti-constituent front," claiming that Congress alone had the power to reform the constitution and that an assembly was "unnecessary."[21] Rallying public support, the new president denounced Congress on his weekly radio program, stating, "We have a reactionary congress with explicit desire of those who believe they have a right to monopolise power to bring the government down."[22] With Correa's approval running in the mid-70s (and Congress' stuck in the mid-teens), the combination of anti-congressional public demonstrations and backroom deals ultimately convinced the legislature to tentatively agree to allow the referendum to go forward. Once the

[19] *LAWR*, December 5, 2006.   [20] *LAWR*, January 2007.
[21] *LAWR*, January 11, 2007.   [22] *LAWR*, February 1, 2007.

referendum was on the agenda, the chief source of disagreement was over whether the constituent assembly would be granted plenipotentiary powers, which potentially could be used to dissolve Congress. The conflict then spilled over to envelope the courts and the Supreme Electoral Tribunal, which dismissed fifty-seven legislators of the 100-member legislature and left the body temporarily inquorate.[23] The interim Congress, known as the "congress de los manteles" (named for the alternate deputies who sought to disguise their identity by wearing handkerchiefs over their heads), quickly began to clash with the executive branch.

By July, following a bitter exchange over a scandal involving his minister of the economy, Ricardo Patiño, Correa openly called for the constituent assembly, once elected, to immediately dissolve the legislature.[24] Meanwhile, the opposition had already begun to float the idea publicly of impeaching Correa.[25] With the decisive victory of Correa's movement, Movimiento Alianza País, in the October elections for the constituent assembly, it was clear that Correa, to use his own terminology, would win "the mother of all battles." Despite Congress' desperate last-minute appeals to the Organization of American States and their refusal to take the usual December recess, within hours of its first meeting the constituent assembly dissolved the legislature.[26]

In a country that had experienced no fewer than eight presidents in less than ten years, and where the president already had significant policy-making powers, there is little doubt that Correa's decision to convoke a constituent assembly and dissolve the opposition-controlled legislature arose in good part from his own fear of being removed. In an interview I conducted with the leader of the opposition party Democracia Popular and former deputy, Diego Ordoñez, I asked explicitly, "Do you think that Correa had some sort of fear that Congress would [treat] him the way that they did his predecessors?" to which he emphatically responded:

> Yes, when the new Congress was established, I used to tell them "the first day you have to say this: President, our hand is stretched out in order to realize the changes this country needs." They didn't do that. Instead, they put on gloves and said, "let's fight." Correa, being the biggest contender here, they were killed ... they should have taken a wiser position.[27]

Reflecting on the constitutional crisis, other politicians expressed similar sentiments. Commenting on Correa's motives and the work of the

---

[23] *LAWR*, March 8, 2007.   [24] *LAWR*, July 2007.   [25] *LAWR*, July 26, 2007.
[26] *LAWR*, December 6 and 13, 2007.   [27] Author interview, July 2008, Quito, Ecuador.

constituent assembly, the former vice president, Rosalia Arteaga, who herself had been deposed by Congress after holding the presidency a mere three days, had this to say:

He [Correa] was so afraid of being overthrown, that was his biggest fear, because he didn't have anyone in Congress. One thing I have to give Correa, he has a great ability ... the congressional tribunal was perfectly managed, a person who did not have even one representative, achieves this ...[28]

In sum, each of the four presidents discussed above made the decision to dissolve Congress not merely to expand his policymaking power but to avoid losing office. In Fujimori's and Serrano's administrations, the opposition in Congress had already opened investigations and had explicitly raised the prospect of impeachment. As Fujimori himself later explained to a group of businessmen, "If I hadn't taken those measures [to dissolve Congress], they would have deposed me" (cited in Kenney, 2004: 207). Likewise, shortly before carrying out his own failed self-coup, Serrano reportedly telephoned the recently impeached president of Venezuela, Carlos Andrés Pérez, proclaiming, "They will not do to me what they did to you."[29] In Correa's case, the president had no representatives in Congress, and executive-legislative relations quickly deteriorated into a struggle over which branch would survive. In Venezuela, Chávez disrupted the institutional order not necessarily because he was under an imminent threat, but because he had extraordinarily good reasons to believe that he would have to confront legislative opponents down the line under circumstances far less propitious for his own survival. All four cases thus comport with the overarching drive to survive logic that stems from the bargaining framework.

5.3 DISCUSSION

When presidents attempt to remake legislatures in their own image, observers frequently conclude that it is purely out of desire to govern their country "as they see fit." Invoking Guillermo O'Donnell's highly influential concept of delegative democracy, the assumption of most postmortem case studies has been that attacks on the legislature, like attacks on the judiciary, the subject of the following chapter, stem largely from Latin American presidents' steadfast refusal to countenance any limits on their power. But,

---

[28] Author interview, July 22 and July 31, 2008, Quito, Ecuador.
[29] *LAWR*, June 10, 1993.

of course, even if we agree that Latin American leaders generally would prefer to rule unfettered, the fact that the vast majority of presidents do not threaten the constitutional order, even when they are in the minority, suggests that this is, at best, only part of the story.

Against the view that such crises indicate that presidents are all powerful, I have argued that this confuses the cause for the effect. The takeaway message here is that legislative crises are triggered instead by presidents who feel cornered and who have the means and ability to lash out first. Simply put, presidential instability, not presidential invincibility, triggers legislative instability. A second and related lesson is that although presidential crises tend to occur with greater frequency in contemporary Latin America than legislative crises, this does not necessarily mean that legislatures are entirely out of the woods. On the contrary, this chapter implies that presidential instability spills over into, rather than substitutes for, other types of institutional instability.

6

Caught in the Cross-Fire?

Inter-Branch Crises and Judicial Instability

It's not [judicial] instability, it's instability of the country; we are a part of the country, that's it.

– Vice President of the Ecuadorian Supreme Court[1]

For observers of Latin American judiciaries, the pattern is all too familiar: courts that begin as mere adjudicators of legislative-executive disputes often end up as helpless targets caught in their own institutional debacles. Whether ruling on corruption scandals involving the administration, determining the legality of the president's ability to convene a constituent assembly, or deciding the constitutionality of the legislature launching an impeachment, courts across the region are routinely drawn into the very sorts of institutional battles that stand to directly threaten the executive's ability to maintain his or her grip on power. Having established that legislative crises in Latin America are triggered, at least in part, by presidents' aversion to being ousted, this chapter turns to explore the related proposition that presidential attacks against the judiciary are fueled by a similar dynamic.

At first glance, this argument may seem superfluous. After all, in each of the legislative crises analyzed in the previous chapter, courts were also targeted. In Peru, the self-coup carried out by Alberto Fujimori in 1992 simultaneously dissolved Congress and called for a total reorganization of the judiciary, which had been dominated by judges seen as loyal to the opposition. Likewise, in Guatemala, Serrano immediately dissolved both the Supreme Court and the Court of Constitutionality during the

---

[1] Author interview with José Vicente Troya, July 2008, Quito, Ecuador.

self-coup, placing under house arrest the head of the Supreme Court along with the Human Rights Ombudsman (Ramiro de Leon Carpio, who would later be president) and head of Congress. In Venezuela, the Supreme Court ultimately caved to pressure from Chávez to allow the national constituent assembly both to marginalize the existing legislature and to dismiss judges accused of corruption and incompetence. Cecelia Sosa Gómez, the Chief Justice of the Supreme Court, famously quipped in response, "The Court simply committed suicide to avoid being assassinated. But the result is the same, it is dead" (*El Universal*, August 25, 1999, cited in Sanchez Urribarri, 2010: 220).

And in Ecuador, the Supreme Court was drawn deeper and deeper into the "mother of all battles" that raged between Correa's administration and the legislature over the formation of the constituent assembly. In the end, the justices were forced to resign shortly after the new constitution was approved in the national referendum held on September 28, 2008.[2]

Given this, it is tempting to infer that the destruction of the courts is merely collateral damage. Once the president bears the cost of disrupting the institutional order by attacking the legislature, there is simply no reason to spare the judiciary.[3] Yet, as this chapter will make clear, even when courts are purged in tandem with legislatures, judges often serve as attractive targets in their own right. Returning to the Peruvian example, Fujimori's ill-will toward the judiciary actually preceded his battles with the legislature. Within his first hundred days in office, the president and members of the National Association of Judges openly quarreled over Fujimori's decision to release unsentenced prisoners accused of minor crimes. In response to the judiciary's objections, Fujimori publicly labeled the judges "jackals and scoundrels" (Kenney, 2004: 132). In another incident, the Supreme Court's controversial decision to drop all charges against Abimael Guzmán, the leader of the Sendero Luminoso, was seen as a direct rebuke of Fujimori's attempt to fight terrorism. Coming on the heels of a broader judicial scandal, which uncovered a pattern of lower court judges both releasing convicted terrorists early and dismissing suspected terrorists without cause, the government increasingly came to

---

[2] According to the terms of the transition, all thirty-one justices from the Supreme Court of Justice were required to tender their resignations within ten days. Subsequently, twenty-one of the original thirty-one members were to be chosen by lottery to serve as interim justices on the new Corte Nacional de Justicia bench until the new procedures for selecting judges could be implemented in the following year. (*LAWR*, November 2008).

[3] I am grateful to an anonymous reviewer for suggesting this argument.

see the judiciary en toto as a dangerous impediment not only to its success in countering terrorism, but also to maintaining Fujimori's grip on power. Indeed, although Fujimori ultimately decided to carry out the self-coup against both branches, for months he had been contemplating a petit coup, which would have left Congress intact and unconstitutionally replaced judges in the judiciary, the Tribunal of Constitutional Guarantees, the National Magistrates Council, and the attorney general's office (Kenny, 2004: 199).

More generally, this chapter argues that judicial manipulation constitutes a distinct tool in the president's arsenal for avoiding removal. The reasoning is straightforward. For although judges, unlike legislators, cannot unilaterally threaten to oust the president, judges are clearly capable of altering the various parameters that affect presidential instability. Thus, when presidents are already at risk, they are much more likely to try to gain control over their courts. At the same time, because judicial manipulation can manifest itself in a multitude of ways, ranging from impeachment and forced resignations to court-packing, and can occur whether the president enjoys a congressional majority or not, singling out courts is often a much easier strategy for presidents than launching a full-blown constitutional coup. This helps make sense of the fact that while legislative instability rarely occurs without judicial instability, the reverse is not true.

By arguing that the threat of presidential instability also drives judicial instability, this chapter sketches out a novel logic of judicial manipulation that sharply departs from conventional explanations. Consider the two leading rational choice explanations of judicial independence: the SOP approach (Ferejohn and Weingast, 1992; Gely and Spiller, 1990; Epstein and Knight, 1998) and the insulation theory (Ramseyer, 1994; Ramseyer and Rasmusen, 1997; Ginsburg, 2003; Finkel, 2008). According to the former, judges are in the strongest position and able to exercise the most independence whenever there is a split between the executive and legislative branches. According to the latter, only when presidents are losing power will they be inclined to imbue courts with independence in order to tie the hands of their successors. Thus, in different ways, both arguments imply that weaker governments breed stronger courts. By highlighting instead how the president's insecurity in office leads him to seize control over the judiciary, this chapter effectively turns that aphorism on its head.

The rest of the chapter unfolds as follows. The next section extends the bargaining framework developed in Chapter 3 to the judiciary. More specifically, I discuss how the court's capacity to affect the various parameters that underlie the legislature's decision to oust presidents transforms judges into targets for both presidents and the opposition alike. The second half of the chapter then returns to the ICLA dataset to explore the multiple testable implications that flow from this new theory of judicial manipulation. Following the offensive strike logic, I show that variation in judicial crises is systematically related to the president's risk of instability and to the costs presidents bear for purging their courts, as captured by presidential powers, timing within the presidential term, the history of past presidential instability, and confidence in the judiciary. Along the way, I rule out multiple alternative hypotheses. The conclusion then explores the broader implications of my findings for how we think about the political underpinnings of judicial independence.

6.1 A NEW THEORY OF JUDICIAL MANIPULATION

Recall from Chapter 3 the core conditions that gave rise to presidential instability. Borrowing from Powell's (1999) influential theory of bargaining in the shadow of power, I showed that increasing presidential powers raises the stakes to the legislative opposition for being out of power. The wider the gap between the president's formal institutional powers and her partisan powers, the more likely it is that the opposition will become dissatisfied and seek to oust the president. In turn, to the extent that presidents can foresee such a gap emerging, they may be tempted to launch a preventive strike against the legislative opposition, effectively removing a potential threat before conditions shift against them. Formally, the legislature's threshold for triggering a presidential crisis can be expressed as $Q < p - d$, where Q represents the scope of the legislature's powers to set policy, p represents the probability that the attempt to oust the president is successful, and d represents the cost to the legislature of carrying out the attack. In turn, the president's threshold for launching a preventive strike against the legislature can similarly be expressed as $d - c > 1 - Q$, where d represents the probability that the president will succeed and c represents the president's cost for the attack.

Using this bargaining framework as an alternative lens through which to view the logic of judicial manipulation, I begin with the observation that in such institutional environments the judiciary matters because of its capacity to influence the parameters that affect the legislature's and executive's calculi for conflict. Of course, in any concrete situation, the court's influence will be bounded. Depending on its jurisdiction, courts can hear only certain types of cases. Overturning precedent is certainly possible, but may be costly. And, of course, legislatures can always pass new laws that get around judicial decisions. That said, as long as courts have the capacity to marginally shift the parameters within the bargaining framework, then both the president and the legislature alike potentially face incentives to control it.

6.1.1 Presidential Powers

Because the main function of courts in a democracy is to interpret the constitution, the judiciary helps shape the scope of executive power (Q in the model). Examples abound of courts that are friendly to the president issuing decisions expanding presidential power, as well as courts that are loyal to the opposition contracting it. As we alluded to in Chapter 3, for instance, in Argentina during the 1990s the recently stacked judiciary allowed the executive to issue bonds to stem the financial crisis, thus expanding Carlos Menem's decree power. A decade later, with the previous administration's court still largely intact, the judges essentially reversed themselves in *Smith*, when they struck down President Duhalde's bid to freeze savings accounts during the 2001 economic meltdown (Helmke 2005: 147–148). Likewise, in Peru prior to the *autogolpe*, the opposition-dominated judiciary repeatedly struck down Fujimori's economic and security policies (Kenny 2004). By contrast, following the self-coup, few of Fujimori's newly appointed judges dared to challenge the government's expansive use of presidential powers, and those that did were swiftly punished.[4] In terms of the executive-legislative bargaining model, courts thus can shift Q, the parameter that represents the president's ability to set policy, either to the right or to the left by ruling on cases that involve the distribution of power between the executive and legislative branches.

6.1.2 Probability of Success

Of course, the observation that presidents value judges who expand their policymaking power is hardly surprising. This assumption lies at the core of the familiar delegative democracy argument espoused by Guillermo O'Donnell (1994) whereby presidents are loathe to tolerate any checks on their power. Yet notice that the main implication of the

---

[4] Most notably, in 1997 the Constitutional Tribunal refused to allow Fujimori to run for a third term, and three of the judges were subsequently impeached. With a fourth judge resigning in protest, the court was left inquorate; Fujimori ran for office and won.

executive-legislative bargaining model is that expanding the president's policymaking power also simultaneously increases the risk to that president. Put differently, moving Q to the right may please a power-hungry president, but it also effectively lowers the legislature's threshold for becoming dissatisfied. Thus, from the standpoint of the president seeking to cling to office, judicial manipulation is not only about expanding constitutional power, but also about affecting the probability of the opposition's success in ousting the president (or p in the core bargaining model).

Most obviously, in countries with single chamber legislatures where high courts are called on to serve as the second chamber in any formal impeachment process, the court profoundly affects whether presidents are ultimately removed from office. In Venezuela, the Supreme Court played this role during the impeachment process that removed Carlos Andres Pérez from office in 1992. In Brazil, the Court served the same function in Collor de Mello's impeachment. More recently, the Guatemalan Supreme Court green-lighted the process for removing Otto Pérez Molina's immunity to stand trial on corruption charges, which ultimately led to the resignation of the president.[5]

Beyond its role as a prosecutorial body, the judiciary can also affect the legislature's probability of successfully removing the executive in other ways. Consider Evo Morales' judicial strategy in Bolivia. Following one of the most surprising presidential elections in Bolivian history, the former cocalero leader swept to power in December 2005, winning the first round with 53.7 percent of the vote and claiming the majority of seats in Congress. Although Morales went on to garner the largest vote share in recent Bolivian history, from the very beginning his presidency was deeply polarizing, particularly along geographic lines. From his decision to nationalize Bolivia's gas reserves to his convocation of a constituent assembly, his first year in office only further exacerbated deep-seated regional tensions and led to increasing demands for autonomy by the richer "Media Luna" region (Lehoucq, 2008).

Indeed, despite the unprecedented majority of the Movimiento al Socialismo in the lower house, in the next few years Morales would go on to face numerous referenda challenging his hold over breakaway regions, as well as his hold on the presidency itself.[6] Midway through

---

[5] *The Guardian*, September 1, 2015.
[6] To give just one example, in September 2007, the governor of Cochabamba, Manfredo Reyes Villa, called for Morales to resign for his incompetence and for leading the country to the brink of civil war. See *LAWR*, September 6, 2007.

his first year in power, the Defense Minister threatened protesters in the antigovernment regions with court action for engaging in "secessionist discourse."[7] After that, courts were asked to adjudicate everything from monetary claims stemming from the government's decision to nationalize the gas and oil industry to corruption charges against opposition politicians, including the former president (Carey 2009), to the legality of Morales' recall referendum.

Not surprisingly, Morales, like his counterparts in Venezuela and Ecuador, quickly realized that he needed to take control over the courts to help thwart challenges both to his policies and to his grip on office. As Castagnola and Peréz-Liñán (2011) describe, almost immediately after Morales took office, justices on both the Supreme Court and the Constitutional Tribunal were pressured to tender their resignations.[8] Criticizing the court's former composition as "tantamount to an a priori sentence against indigenous people,"[9] Morales unilaterally used his decree powers to fill the new vacancies on the bench rather than employ the standard method of selection (via a joint session of both houses of Congress). By March 2008, only a single judge, Silvia Salame Farjat, was left on the tribunal.[10] Meanwhile, the government also initiated several impeachment proceedings against remaining Supreme Court members for allegedly protecting the opposition. By purging the opposition's judiciary, Morales ultimately succeeded in foreclosing one of the opposition's most important tools for challenging his efforts to control the constituent

---

[7] *LAWR*, September 12, 2006.

[8] Part of this early wave of resignations arose, no doubt, from the skirmishes between the executive and the judiciary over the latter's alleged failure to punish corruption associated with past administrations (*LAWR*, April 25, 2006). Most notably, Morales lambasted the Supreme Court for failing to process cases dealing with the previous interim administration's controversial decision to hand over surface-to-air missiles to the United States for destruction. According to one report, Morales explicitly threatened the judiciary, stating, "If the judges did not prove to the people that they were devoted to doing 'justice and not simply trying to protect the corrupt' then by the time the constituent assembly is called, they may find themselves out of jobs" (*LAWR*, April 25, 2006). For its part, the Constitutional Tribunal was undone by its opposition to Morales' decision to appoint new Supreme Court justices by decree. One month after the Constitutional Tribunal's rather bold decision curtailing the president's decree, the government brought charges against four of the five justices for "perverting the course of justice" (*LAWR*, May 24, 2007).

[9] *LAWR*, January 2007.

[10] Although Justice Farjat could issue only nonbinding decrees, over the next two years she used her post to challenge the government, ruling, for instance, in July 2008 that the recall referendum against Morales and the opposition governors should be cancelled (Castagnola and Pérez-Liñán, 2011: 301). A little less than a year later, she finally stepped down.

assembly. As Lehoucq (2008) notes, the constitutional reform process triggered enormous opposition and surely would have prompted litigation by the opposition had the Constitutional Tribunal still been operative.

Turning to Ecuador, yet another way in which courts can shape the probability of presidential ousters is exemplified by the tactics employed during Lucio Gutiérrez's short-lived administration (2003–2005). With Gutiérrez's own Patriotic Society Party holding just six of the 100 congressional seats, the president blatantly used the judiciary as a bargaining chip with its allies (Mejía Acosta and Polga-Hecimovich, 2010). By early 2004, Gutiérrez faced a mounting series of criminal charges ranging from covering up corruption within the administration to accepting campaign contributions for his party from drug traffickers and foreign parties.[11] As demands for the president's impeachment grew and his relationship with his then-current coalition partner, the PSC, became increasingly strained, Gutiérrez began a series of negotiations with the PRE and the Partido Renovador Institucional Acción Nacional (PRIAN) to fundamentally restructure the nation's high courts.

Starting with a new round of appointments at the Constitutional Tribunal and the Supreme Electoral Tribunal in November 2004, which clearly targeted PSC judges, Gutiérrez promised that the newly designated judges were only temporary replacements until a referendum to fully "depoliticize" the judiciary could be held.[12] A little less than a month later, however, the administration again went after the Supreme Court, replacing all thirty-one justices in one fell swoop. Despite the government's claim that the tenure of the Supreme Court justices had simply run out at the end of January 2003, news leaked that the government had cut a quid pro quo deal with the PRE in which the new court would drop charges pending against exiled president Bucaram in exchange for the PRE's efforts to block impeachment charges against Gutiérrez.[13] The new so-called Pinchi Corte, which was named after the nickname of one of Bucaram's closest childhood friends, the new Chief Justice Guillermo Castro, quickly seemed to validate critics' concerns: the Court's very first decision was to withdraw the arrest warrants against Bucaram and allow his return to Ecuador, thereby salvaging – albeit temporarily – Gutiérrez's bid to retain power.

---

[11] *LAWR*, April 20, 2004.   [12] *LAWR*, November 30, 2004.
[13] *LAWR*, December 14, 2004.

6.1.3 Costs

In addition to affecting Q and p, courts can also influence the legislature's cost of an attack by affecting the president's popularity. Most obviously, judicial manipulation itself might jeopardize or help consolidate the president's public support, thereby influencing the legislature's threshold for conflict. Returning to the Gutiérrez example, purging and packing the Ecuadorian Supreme Court may have assuaged the PRE, but such obvious institutional manipulation also triggered a massive outpouring of opposition across a range of social and political actors, which ultimately led to the president's ouster.

For the most part, however, presidents who target the judiciary seem to have skillfully played on the public's dissatisfaction with elite institutions. Returning again to the Andean experiences, judicial manipulation qua judicial reform has proved immensely popular. Prior to Chávez's election, for instance, the Venezuelan judiciary was widely considered one of the country's most corrupt and inefficient institutions. During the 1990s, a best-selling book entitled *How Much to Buy a Judge?* described major law firms participating in informal networks that enabled their clients to purchase favorable rulings. Attesting to the political impunity that flourished under the old system, a prominent Venezuelan lawyer lamented,

The political parties handed out all the appointments ... each judge owes his job to political interests ... If a son of a politician commits a crime, it is very difficult to punish him.[14]

Meanwhile, enormous case backlogs meant that claims made by ordinary citizens tended to languish in the court system for years, if not decades (Hammergren, 2007). Summarizing these problems, a 1996 study by the Lawyers Committee for Human Rights concluded that the country's judiciary

symbolized all that had gone wrong with Venezuela's political system. The roots of the crisis in the judiciary intertwine several areas: political interference, corruption, institutional neglect, and the failure to provide access to justice for the vast part of the Venezuelan population.[15]

---

[14] "Chávez continues dramatic campaign to end judicial corruption," *Miami Herald*, May 1, 2000.
[15] "Halfway to reform: The World Bank and the Venezuelan justice system," August 1996 (cited in Wilpert, 2007: 44).

Building on this discontent, Chávez successfully pitched his attack on the Venezuelan judiciary as part and parcel of a broader plan to eliminate the last vestiges of the traditional Punto Fijo system and the massive corruption associated with it. Likewise, Fujimori's decision to purge the Peruvian judiciary also proved to be hugely popular. By the time of the coup, fully 89 percent of Peruvians approved of Fujimori's decision to intervene in the judiciary (Kenney, 2004: 228). And during the Morales administration's assault on the judiciary, the government released a fifty-page document, entitled "Towards a New Justice System in Bolivia," which labeled the judiciary as the country's "most corrupt" institution.[16] Polls taken by Transparency International that same year indicate that more than 80 percent of Bolivian respondents shared the government's view.

6.1.4 Testable Implications

In sum, whether by expanding the scope of presidential powers, limiting the strength of the opposition, and/or helping the president curry favor with the public, manipulating the judiciary potentially helps presidents at risk avert being ousted themselves. As a result, in institutional environments that are predisposed to such instability, the stakes for capturing the courts will be that much higher. Thus, if judicial manipulation is rooted in the president's fear of removal, then several of the hypotheses from the previous chapter on legislative crises naturally extend to judicial crises.

Let me begin, however, with the one hypothesis that does require modification: the core bargaining hypothesis. Recall that in previous chapters the onset of crises depended on the interaction of the president's de jure and de facto powers. By contrast, I would argue that judicial crises instead depend only on the distribution of de jure power. The reasoning is twofold. On the one hand, as with presidential and legislative crises, if minority presidents are more likely than majority presidents to face a threat of removal, then they should also have the greatest incentive to target the courts. On the other hand, however, the institutional rules suggest that minority presidents will tend to have a much tougher time succeeding in replacing the judiciary, at least if the legislature is still intact. Certainly, formal impeachment and court-packing requires at least majority control

---

[16] *LAWR*, May 24, 2007.

over the legislature to succeed. Therefore, assuming that these two counter-vailing effects – incentives and ability – essentially cancel each other out, then partisan status should be less relevant for explaining judicial manipulation than it is for explaining the other two types of crises. This leads to the first hypothesis.

H1 (Revised Bargaining Theory): The likelihood of a judicial crisis increases as the president's constitutional powers grow, regardless of whether the president is in the minority.

Notice that this hypothesis runs directly counter to two prominent alternative hypotheses. First, the argument that more powerful presidents are more likely to launch judicial crises than weaker presidents contradicts the delegative democracy logic. A key – albeit heretofore untested – implication of that argument is that because constitutionally weaker presidents would benefit marginally more from friendly courts than constitutionally stronger presidents, we should see presidential attacks on the judiciary decreasing as formal presidential powers increase. This can be expressed in the following alternative hypothesis.

H2 (Delegative Democracy): The likelihood of a judicial crisis decreases as the president's constitutional powers grow, regardless of whether the president is in the minority.

Second, notice that in contrast to the revised bargaining theory, the standard SOP account focuses solely on the distribution of partisan power, not constitutional power. Put differently, if the SOP account provides the better explanation for judicial crises, then the probability of judicial manipulation will rise among majority presidents irrespective of their constitutional power.[17] This then leads to the third hypothesis.

H3 (Separation of Powers): The likelihood of a judicial crisis decreases if the president is in the minority, regardless of the president's constitutional power.

The next two hypotheses adhere directly to the preventive logic laid out for legislative crises whereby a president's expectations regarding her risk

---

[17] I want to distinguish between a separation of powers framework that assumes judges have complete information and one that does not. In the former, judges adjust their decision-making to please the majority, and punishment remains off the equilibrium path. In the latter, we might expect that judges do not know precisely the preferences of the unified government, which may lead to more judicial crises. H3 is geared toward this second understanding of separation of power systems.

of removal also serve to heighten the likelihood of a judicial crisis. Specifically, if the shadow of presidential instability extends to judicial crises, then past episodes of presidential instability in a given country and past shifts in presidential popularity in a given country should matter. This can be stated as testable hypotheses.

H4 (Past Presidential Instability): The likelihood of a judicial crisis increases with a history of previous attacks on presidents in a given country.

H5 (Past Presidential Popularity): The likelihood of a judicial crisis increases with a history of predecessors losing popular support over the course of their term in a given country.

In addition, if judicial manipulation by presidents is designed to increase the cost to the legislature of going after the president, then public confidence in the judiciary should be negatively correlated with judicial crises ex ante. This dovetails with the key insight that comes out of an important literature in comparative judicial politics (see, e.g., Vanberg, 2005; Staton, 2010), which contends that politicians are less likely to attack courts that enjoy public support and more likely to go after courts that do not. Likewise, if presidents are trying to maximize the stream of benefits of a loyal judiciary, then, all else equal, they should target courts earlier in their terms as opposed to later. Turning to parties, to the extent that the age of the president's party is a proxy for party strength, then party age should also be negatively correlated with judicial crises. In the case of courts, stronger parties also make it that much more likely that the president will face judges who are already sympathetic for the simple reason that members of the presidential party are more likely to have had an opportunity to shape the composition of the existing court.[18] Taken together, the foregoing observations can be summarized as the following three testable implications.

H6 (Judicial Confidence): The likelihood of a judicial crisis decreases as public support for the judiciary increases.

H7 (Timing): The likelihood of a judicial crisis decreases with the amount of time the administration has been in power.

H8 (Party Age): The likelihood of a judicial crisis increases as the age of the president's party decreases.

---

[18] Thus, if we find an effect of *Party Age* on judicial crises, it is unclear whether this lends support to the parties-as-constraints mechanism or to the compatibility argument.

The last hypotheses point to two additional types of instability spill-overs that are specific to courts. Intuitively, for instance, we might imagine that presidents whose predecessors stacked the court will be that much more motivated to repeat the process when they come to power, regardless of whether they themselves are at risk of removal. This, after all, was precisely the justification invoked by Carlos Menem in Argentina, who, just before stacking the Supreme Court, famously quipped, "Why should I be the only Argentine president not to have my own court?" This implies a self-sustaining cycle of judicial instability whereby newly elected governments expect to play a defection strategy and judicial dependence becomes the steady state equilibrium (cf. Ramseyer, 1994; Helmke and Rosenbluth, 2009).[19] Although this reasoning is certainly not antithetical to my risk mitigation story, notice that it does hint at a distinct mechanism for repeated bouts of judicial instability, which is compatible with the argument that presidents simply prefer compliant courts. This can be stated as follows.

H9 (Predecessor Judicial Crises): The likelihood of judicial crises in the current administration increases if the predecessor government has successfully manipulated the court.

Last but not least, the president's manipulation of the courts also sets the stage for opposition legislative attacks against courts. Precisely because courts potentially enhance the executive's powers, it makes sense that opposition legislators will seek to regain control over the judiciary as quickly as they can. Following Menem's court-packing in 1990, for instance, opposition legislators from the Radical party repeatedly threatened to impeach the president's cronies on the bench (Baglini and D'Ambrosio, 1993; Octavio de Jesus and Ruscelli, 1998: 27). Ultimately, in order to get constitutional reforms passed would that allow him to stand for reelection, Menem signed the Pacto de Olivos with the opposition in 1994, which led two of his five justices to resign (Barra and Cavagna Martinez). With the majority of the court still controlled by Menem's appointees, however, in 1998 the opposition alliance in the legislature compiled another dossier to document the dereliction and favoritism of the Argentine Supreme Court. In Argentina, both legislative attacks were thus largely reactions to the

---

[19] To the extent that previous attacks on the court also endogenously lower the court's legitimacy, it will also be that much easier for the current president to remake the court in his or her own image. See Chapter 7.

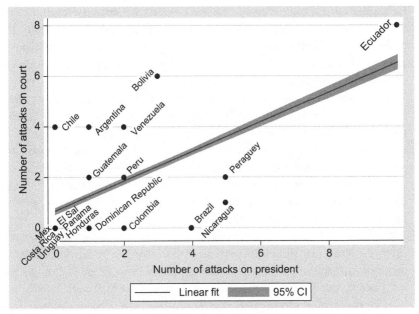

FIGURE 6.1: Bivariate relationship between presidential and judicial crises.

president's early offensive attack on the court. To the extent that legislative attacks on courts elsewhere are triggered by a similar mechanism, then this suggests that such crises may form the last link in the unfolding chain of institutional instability that starts with the basic bargaining failure between executives and legislatures. This can be stated as the following final testable implication.

H10 (Legislative-Judicial Crises): The likelihood of a legislative attack on the courts increases if the current executive has previously manipulated the judiciary.

6.2 PATTERNS OF PRESIDENTIAL AND JUDICIAL INSTABILITY

Broadly in line with the theoretical argument of this chapter that the risk of presidential crises begets judicial crises, one of the clearest empirical patterns uncovered in Chapter 2 is that presidential and judicial crises often do go hand in hand. To see this bivariate relationship more clearly, Figure 6.1 simply regresses the total number of judicial crises instigated by presidents on the total number of presidential crises instigated by legislatures for each country. Moving from the country-level to the administration-level, basic bivariate statistical analysis shows that the odds of a president who does not suffer a crisis attacking the judiciary are around 15 percent, while the odds that a president who does suffer a crisis will target the court rises to 41 percent.

Yet from the standpoint of evaluating my theory, there are several reasons not to make too much of the correlation between the actual number of presidential crises and judicial crises. Indeed, as Figure 6.1 and Table 6.1 show, there are plenty of instances in which one type of attack occurs without the other. Specifically, the off-diagonal corners of Table 6.1 contain as many or more administrations in which a presidential crisis occurred without a judicial crisis (upper-right hand corner) and vice versa (lower-left hand corner).

Consider first the twenty-one cases that comprise the former category. One plausible explanation is that among the administrations that fall into the upper-right corner compared with those in the upper-left corner, the president may have had less reason to fear an attack. Indeed, if we return to the core model of presidential crises estimated in Chapter 4, we should find that these are the cases that are more likely to be underpredicted by the model. Setting the threshold at 50 percent, this is precisely what we find. Of the ten cases that are underpredicted by the core model, nine of them are located in the upper-right corner (Alemán, Balaguer, Chamoro, Collor, Cubas, Lula, Ortega, Samper, and Sarney). Conversely, we also see the highest rate of overpredicted presidential attacks among the administrations located in the lower-left hand corner, suggesting that these unchallenged presidents might have nevertheless feared being removed and lashed out at their courts accordingly.[20] What

---

[20] Specifically, 38 percent of the administrations in the lower-left category were overpredicted by the core model at the 50 percent threshold (Alarcón, Carpio, Duhalde, Menem, and Sanchez de Lozada), compared with 31 percent of administrations in the lower-right cell. For the remaining cases located in the upper-right cell, the reasons presidents might have failed to purge their courts before coming under attack themselves are more idiosyncratic, but certainly not incompatible with the overarching logic that manipulation occurs by presidents who are seeking to avert risk. For instance, some presidents who failed to launch attacks were on their second or even third term (Balaguer and Fujimori), whereas others were serving an interim term or were attacked immediately after coming to power (Mahuad and Sanchez de Lozada). In the former cases, presidents had already had ample opportunity to remake the courts in their own image, whereas in the latter they had little time to do so. However, notice that the average gap between coming to power and attacking the courts is actually slightly lower for the thirteen administrations (2.2 years) in the upper-left corner compared with the sixteen administrations (2.5 years) located in the upper-right cell that were not serving a second term by the presidential crisis model.

TABLE 6.1: *Presidential Crises and Judicial Crises*

	Judicial Crisis	No Judicial Crisis
Presidential Crisis	Bolaños 2004, 2005/2004 Bucaram 1997/1996 Chávez 2002/2002, 2003 Cordero 1987/1985 Correa 2007/2007 Duarte 2005/2003 Durán-Ballén 1995/1994 Fujimori 1991/1991 Gutiérrez 2004, 2005/2003, 2004, 2005 Paz Zamora 1990/1990 Pérez 1992/1992 Serrano 1993/1993 Wasmosy 1996/1993	Alemán 1997 Balaguer 1994 Borja 1990;1992 Cardoso 1999 Chamoro 1995 Collor 1992 Cubas 1998 De La Rúa 2001 Fujimori 2000 Gonzales Macchi 2001, 2002 Lula 2005 Mahuad 1999 Ortega 2007 Palacio 2005 Pastrana 2000 Samper 1995 Sánchez de Lozada 2003 Sarney 1987 Siles 1985
No Presidential Crisis	Alarcón 1997 Alfonsín 1987 Aylwin 1991, 1992 De León 1993 Chávez 1999 Duhalde 2002 Frei 1997, 1999 Fujimori 1997 Kirchner 2003 Menem 1989 Morales 2006, 2007, 2008 Paz Estenssoro 1987 Sánchez de Lozada 1993	

is more, the thirteen cases located in this category may be entirely consistent with the offensive strike logic outlined above, insofar as these judicial attacks may have actually helped to avert a presidential crisis. For example, it is easy to overlook the fact that one of the main factors leading Carlos Menem to pack the court was his concern with preventing the possibility of impeachment down the line. As the *Latin American*

Weekly Report put it, "No chance here of a successful impeachment move, even if the corruption scandals which have involved the President's inner circle ever touch him personally."[21] Yet because we can never know whether such counterfactuals are valid, the theoretical framework developed in this chapter demands that we move beyond basic correlations among presidential crises and judicial crises and toward an estimation strategy that considers explicitly how the risk that presidents face affects their propensity to manipulate their courts.

6.3 PREDICTING JUDICIAL CRISES: A STATISTICAL ANALYSIS

To explore systematically the multiple testable implications that come from extending the bargaining framework to courts, this section presents the results from a series of rare events logit models. Here, the dependent variable *Judicial Crises* takes on a value of 1 for all observations in which the executive threatens to alter or alters the composition of the high court (s) through impeachment, forced resignation, dissolution, or court packing, and 0 otherwise. Given the overlap between judicial and legislative crises (e.g., Fujimori's *autogolpe* targeted both institutions simultaneously), I check all of the results using only the isolated judicial crises. This robustness check ensures that the results for the judiciary are not driven by the executive's decision to attack the legislature, which has already been accounted for in the previous chapter. The independent variables are constructed in a manner identical to the previous empirical chapters, unless otherwise specified.

To assess the first three hypotheses, I start with the baseline interactive model used to predict the likelihood of a legislative attack on the president and vice versa, which includes measures for the president's constitutional powers, partisan powers, their interaction, and the variable *Protest*. Following the logic elaborated in the previous section, here I expect that increasing the president's de jure powers should also increase the likelihood of a judicial crisis, but that the president's de facto powers should have no independent or conditional effect (H1). This reasoning stems from the observation that in the case of judicial purges, the president's incentives to target the courts and her ability to do so cut in opposite directions with respect to minority status. This expectation obviously stands in stark contrast to a version of the standard SOP model, which

---

[21] *LAWR*, October 15, 1992.

TABLE 6.2: *Judicial Crises and Risk of Presidential Removal*

	Model 6.1	Model 6.2	Model 6.3
Minority President	0.55		
	(1.13)		
Presidential Power	0.22**		
	(0.09)		
Minority × *Power*	−0.05		
	(0.10)		
Protest	0.22***		
	(0.07)		
Past Removals		0.35***	
		(0.07)	
Past Popularity_Gain			−0.002
			(0.003)
Constant	−4.90***	−3.24***	−2.59***
	(1.08)	(0.35)	(0.53)
N	454	474	105

* $p < 0.1$,
** $p < 0.05$,
*** $p < 0.01$.

predicts that judicial independence decreases among majority presidents regardless of their formal powers (H3). Likewise, the prediction also departs from the conventional wisdom associated with the delegative democracy account in which presidents pack courts merely in order to expand their own policymaking powers; were this the case, we would expect judicial crises to decrease with presidential powers (H2).

The results contained in Model 6.1 and graphed in Figure 6.2 tend to support the first hypothesis and help us to rule out the second and third hypotheses. Although the fact that only the constituent coefficient for *Power* is significant suggests that the effect is limited to majority governments, the graph shows that substantively, the probability of judicial crises increases from less than 1 percent among the weakest presidents to roughly 20 percent among the strongest, regardless of whether the president is in the minority or majority.[22]

These results are robust to estimating the model on the subset of isolated judicial crises, thereby to dropping the five cases in which presidents simultaneously attacked both the courts and the legislature

---

[22] The graph is generated without including *Protest* in this statistical model. Note that the results do not change in any meaningful way if we include the variable.

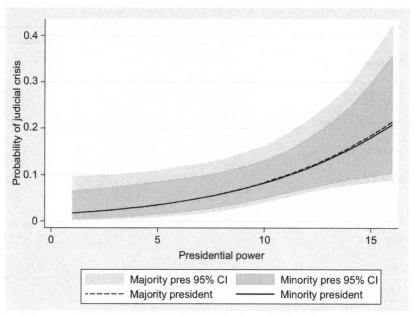

FIGURE 6.2: Predicted probability of judicial crises by presidential power among minority and majority presidents.

(Fujimori, 1991; Serrano, 1993; De León, 1993; Chávez, 1999; Correa, 2007) and to dropping Ecuador, which has the largest single number of judicial crises (1985, 1994, 1996, 1997, 2003, 2004, 2005, 2007).

Turning to the president's expectations about threats to her survival, I again employ the two significant measures used in Chapter 5, *Past Removals* and *Past Popularity_Gain*, to explore their effects on the probability that the president will launch a judicial crisis. Recall that the former count variable measures the number of previous leaders in a given country who have been removed or subjected to threats of removal by Congress for each administration. The latter variable measures the difference in the previous administration's popularity at the beginning and at the end of their presidents' terms. The idea behind this second measure is that if previous presidents have experienced huge drops in support, their successors might believe that they will also lose popularity and thus be that much more vulnerable to legislative attacks.

Starting with *Past Removals*, Model 6.2 and Figure 6.3 show that the history of presidential crises does indeed have a strong positive effect on the likelihood of a judicial crisis (H4). Here, the probability of a judicial crisis starts at less than 5 percent with no previous experiences

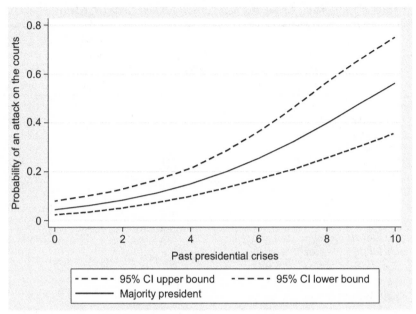

FIGURE 6.3: Predicted probability of judicial crises by past presidential crises.

of presidential instability and jumps to over 50 percent for environments that have experienced the highest number of previous presidential crises.[23] By contrast, there is little discernible effect from swings in the previous president's popularity (H5). Two factors may be responsible. The first is that the lack of data on presidential popularity means that we are losing more than three-quarters of all observations and more than half of the judicial crises. The second factor is that popularity swings are obviously a much less direct measure than past ousters. Thus, it is not entirely clear whether the result challenges the hypothesis or the validity of the measure.

The next set of testable implications (shown in Table 6.3) revolves around the costs faced by presidents who target courts. Although limited, the cross-national public opinion data available from the Latinobarómetro between 1995 and 2008 are used to construct the variable *Judicial*

---

[23] These results continue to hold when we expand the number of judicial crises to include all thirty-three cases and are just shy of significance if we recode the independent variable as a dummy variable representing whether the previous administration experienced a presidential crisis or not. The results, however, are not robust to dropping Ecuador.

Caught in the Cross-Fire?

TABLE 6.3: *Judicial Crises Instigated by Presidents and Legislatures*

	Model 6.4	Model 6.5	Model 6.6	Model 6.7	Model 6.8 Legislative Court Attacks)	Model 6.9
Minority President						1.65 (1.17)
Presidential Power						0.28** (0.11)
Minority × Power						−0.23* (0.12)
Protest						0.14** (0.07)
Past Removals						0.30*** (0.09)
Judicial Confidence (lag)	−0.02** (0.01)					
Party Age			−0.02** (0.01)			−0.27** (0.13)
Term Year		−0.42*** (0.14)				−0.38*** (0.13)
Predecessor Attack				−0.46 (0.49)		−1.52** (0.67)
Judicial Crisis 2					0.81* (0.46)	
Constant	−1.06 (0.69)	−1.66*** (0.48)	−1.87*** (0.47)	−2.72*** (0.35)	−3.91*** (0.40)	−3.70*** (1.33)
N	227	474	459	474	474	454

* $p < 0.1$,
** $p < 0.05$,
*** $p < 0.01$.

Confidence_Lag.[24] If the theoretical expectations derived from the bargaining framework are borne out, then we should find a negative relationship between public support for the judiciary and judicial crises. The results contained in Model 6.4 largely accord with this. Despite the large confidence intervals due to a lack of data, Figure 6.4 reveals that there is

---

[24] As in the previous chapters, I generated average confidence scores for the judiciary by multiplying the percentage of respondents in each category and then adding them together as follows: "a lot" × 2 + "some" × 1 + "a little" × − 1 + "none" × − 2.

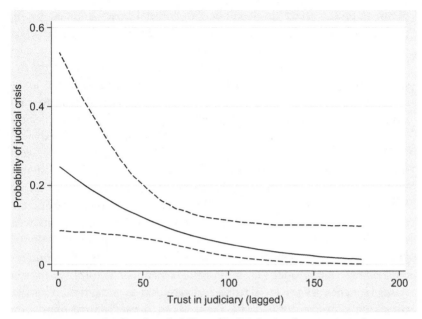

FIGURE 6.4: Predicted probability of judicial crises by trust in judiciary.

indeed a steady decline in the likelihood of a judicial crisis as confidence in the courts increases (H6).

Along similar lines, I also explore whether timing and the age of the president's party can help us to predict the onset of judicial crises. As in the previous chapter, I expect that if presidents are largely following a preventive strategy, then they will try to purge and pack their courts as quickly as possible. As with legislative crises, this is exactly what we see: the coefficient in Model 6.5 is negative and significant (H7). Substantively, the probability of judicial crises ranges from roughly 10 percent in the first year of an administration and declines to less than 1 percent in the seventh year. Turning to *Party Age*, the results are also in line with my expectations. Here, we again see a negative significant relationship (H8).

Last but not least, I address the question of whether previous attacks on the judiciary independently breed subsequent judicial crises. Likewise, to the extent that presidents have been able to gain control over the courts, we might anticipate that the incentives for opposition legislators to try to replace judges also increase. To begin to assess whether the Menem experience occurs more broadly in Latin America, I use the ICLA dataset to explore (1) whether judicial crises initiated by the president that occur at time t affect the likelihood of judicial crises initiated by her predecessor occurring at time $t + 1$, and (2) whether judicial crises initiated by the president affect the likelihood of judicial crises initiated by the opposition legislature during the same administration. In the first specification, the dependent variable remains the same as in the above analyses. In the second specification, I switch the ordered dyad to compare the eleven separate judicial crises that were launched by the legislative opposition against the remaining "noncases" included in this dyad.[25]

The results reported in Models 6.7 and 6.8 suggest that if such traps occur, they are strictly limited to the legislative branch. Menem aside, systematic analysis reveals that most executive attacks on the judiciary are not driven simply by previous instances of judicial manipulation (H9). In other words, whether previous presidents were themselves removed from office (H4) is far more meaningful than if previous presidents merely packed their own courts. By contrast, the results from Model 6.8, where the dependent variable is judicial crises launched by the legislature, indicate that presidential attacks on courts do significantly increase the odds of the legislative opposition trying to reverse the consequences. However, even here, the substantive effects are quite limited. Indeed, if we calculate the marginal effects there is only a slight change in the probability of legislative-led attack on the courts whether the executive has remade the court or not. Thus, presidential instability cascades, but it cascades only so far.

Finally, turning to the full model of presidential attacks on courts (Model 6.9), which is estimated using all of the variables except those based on the Latinobarómetro data, the results remain largely intact. *Presidential Power*, *Protest*, and *Past Removals* continue to be positive and significant, whereas *Term Year* stays negative and significant. The only noticeable differences lie with the interaction term for *Minority**-*Power* and *Predecessor Attack*. In the former case, graphing the interaction reveals that when all of the other factors are included, minority presidents are somewhat less likely to launch judicial crises than their majority counterparts. But, in contrast to a conventional SOP argument, the likelihood does not decline in any meaningful way as their constitutional power increases.[26] With respect to *Predecessor Attack*,

---

[25] The eleven cases in which the legislative opposition initiated an attack on the judiciary include Honduras, 1985; Uruguay, 1985; Ecuador, 1990; Argentina, 1993; Nicaragua, 1995 and 2003; Chile, 1996; Argentina, 1998; Peru, 1998; and Paraguay, 2006 and 2007.

[26] See the replication file available online at http://www.gretchenhelmke.com/data.html.

notice that the coefficient is now significant but in the opposite direction predicted by the penultimate hypothesis. Thus, the results of the full model, if anything, further underscore the plausibility of the risk mitigation strategy versus the simple tit-for-tat norm of judicial manipulation.

6.4 DISCUSSION

Taken together, this chapter makes several new contributions. First and foremost, I have provided an argument for why the threat of presidential instability does not just boomerang onto the legislature, but also spills over onto the courts. As such, we get a similar set of expectations about the factors that trigger both types of attacks on horizontal accountability, but the logic driving judicial crises is somewhat different. Whereas legislatures can directly threaten to remove presidents, the role that courts play is both more subtle and varied. Depending on their jurisdiction, judges can help tilt the playing field on which the executive-legislative bargaining game occurs, by altering the distribution of policymaking powers, as well as the cost and probabilities associated with presidential instability. Thus, to the extent that presidents at risk wish to remain in power, they have every reason to manipulate their courts.[27] And although the evidence is more muted, the chapter also finds some support of a third type of spillover in which opposition legislatures react to executive manipulation of the courts, setting off a new round of judicial instability.

This chapter also speaks to a vast literature on judicial independence. On the one hand, the theoretical framework advanced here builds on recent positive political theories of judicial independence that emphasize the importance of public support or judicial legitimacy (Vanberg 2005; Carrubba 2009). Although the emphasis on such costs is only one component of my theory, the empirical results presented in this chapter provide the first systematic cross-national evidence that public confidence in the courts serves to shield the judiciary. On the other hand, the findings from this chapter also challenge several other existing theories of judicial independence. Specifically, contra the conventional wisdom associated with a wide range of arguments, I find little evidence that presidents attack courts merely in order to expand their own policymaking powers, increase their chances of getting a loyal court, or simply because their

---

[27] Add to this the fact that roughly a third of all Latin American presidents are put on trial after leaving office and the incentives to pack the courts are even greater (Helmke, 2016).

predecessors did so. Likewise, I find little support for at least one version of the SOP approach, which implies that unified government should increase the probability of judicial crises. Last but not least, my results related to the president's uncertainty about remaining in office also cut directly against the well-known insulation story. Whereas proponents of that theory expect that politicians will be more likely to imbue courts with judicial independence at the end of their term as uncertainty about their fates increases, I expect that uncertainty about whether they can complete their terms at all leads politicians to manipulate courts as quickly as they can.

A final ramification of my argument hints at a novel, if disturbing, connection between the so-called judicialization of politics and the politicization of the judiciary. Extending Toharia's finding (1975) that sometimes courts are independent precisely because they have no power, here the implication is that as courts gain the ability to exercise more influence and political actors become more likely to litigate their conflicts, the stakes of politicians controlling the court rise accordingly. This has clearly been the case for leaders such as Morales, who have unabashedly used the courts to prosecute their political enemies, but it also rings true for leaders such as Correa and Chávez, who feared that their opponents would do the same. Contra Hamilton, Madison, and Jay (1961 [1787]), this implies that expanding a court's jurisdiction and/or increasing judicial tenure may actually yield more political attacks against the judiciary, not fewer, particularly if leaders are themselves at risk.[28]

---

[28] Helmke and Staton (2010) make a similar argument about the countervailing effects of tenure and jurisdiction on the likelihood of inter-branch crises, but they highlight the conflicting imperatives that such institutional protections pose for judges, rather than for politicians.

7

Conclusion

When democratic institutions work, political elites tend to resolve their differences through bargaining and compromise. When institutions fail, inter-branch bargaining breaks down and institutional crises reign. While such crises continue to beset contemporary Latin America – witness the removal of Honduran President Manuel Zelaya in June 2009, the accelerated impeachment of Fernando Lugo in Paraguay in 2012, the sudden resignation of Otto Molina Pérez in Guatemala in 2015, the impeachment trial against Dilma Rousseff in Brazil in 2016, or ongoing attempts by the opposition to remove Nicolás Maduro in Venezuela – institutional instability is hardly limited to the contemporary era, nor to the region.

Although the vast majority of Latin American presidents prior to the 1980s fell in military coups, impeachments by the legislature were carried out in Panama (1955), and self-coups took place in Uruguay (1933, 1942), Panama (1946), Colombia (1949), Honduras (1954), and Ecuador (1970).[1] Beyond Latin America, inter-branch crises continue to grab headlines. Since 2010, leaders have faced impeachment in Romania (2012), Thailand (2015), and South Africa (2016); legislatures have been closed in Egypt (2012) and Nepal (2012); and assaults against judicial independence have taken place in Hungary (2011), Sri Lanka (2013), Cambodia (2014), and Poland (2015).

---

[1] See Pérez-Liñán (2007: 52–55).

7.1 SUMMARY

For scholars of democratic institutions, inter-branch crises pose a series of important puzzles. On the empirical side, following the third wave of democratic transitions that crested in the region during the 1980s, the overall incidence of such crises has been stubbornly constant over the last three decades. This persistence is problematic for proponents of democratic consolidation insofar as it clearly undermines the assumption that institutions are prone to gradually improve as long as democratic regimes endure. But the degree of cross-sectional and institutional variation that this book has uncovered also suggests that standard arguments made by critics of consolidation about why political institutions in the region uniformly fail can take us only so far. The facts demand a more fine-grained set of theoretical tools to help us understand why only certain countries and certain institutions are prone to this sort of institutional instability.

On the theoretical side, inter-branch crises pose a familiar dilemma in which political elites ostensibly would benefit from reaching a deal with one another, but nevertheless end up waging a costly institutional battle. If we concede that political actors are rational in the basic sense that they seek to maximize their utility, then we need an approach that explains why presidents at risk of being removed do not simply adjust their behavior to appease their legislative opponents and vice versa. After all, according to classic and contemporary SOP theories, this is precisely how checks and balances should function in equilibrium. Sanctions such as impeachment should serve primarily as deterrents; inter-branch crises should be the proverbial dogs that never bark. And yet in Latin America such crises often occur, and occur repeatedly.

To explain why, I have drawn on formal theories of noncooperative bargaining developed in the international relations literature to account for the onset of inter-state war. Adapting Powell's (1999) theory of bargaining in the shadow of power to inter-branch crises, I have analyzed how the gap between the president's de facto and de jure powers affects the likelihood of different types of inter-branch crises. Ultimately, this approach advances the existing literature on institutions in several important ways. First, whereas previous executive-legislative models (Cox and Morgenstern, 2002) focus exclusively on how constitutionally powerful presidents respond to being in the legislative minority, here I expanded the bargaining scenario to include the legislature's reaction. In a nutshell, I argued that whenever the president's formal powers outstrip his or her partisan powers, not only will the president have an incentive to "go it alone," but the legislative opposition will face heightened incentives to get rid of the president who does so. Of course, if presidents knew with certainty what they would need to cede in order to placate the legislative opposition, the bargaining problem could easily be alleviated. In a more realistic context marked by asymmetric information, however, presidents often do not quite know where the opposition's threshold lies; thus, presidential crises are that much more likely to ensue as the gap in their powers increases.

A second and related contribution of this approach lies in how we think about modeling empirically the underlying causes of institutional crises. Consider presidential crises. Over the last decade, a growing number of studies of presidential removals in Latin America and beyond have highlighted the vulnerability of presidents in the face of minority governments, social protests, scandals, and economic crises(Carey, 2003; Hinojosa and Pérez-Liñán, 2003; Valenzuela, 2004; Mainwaring and Pérez-Liñán, 2005; Hochstetler, 2006; Negretto, 2006; Pérez-Liñán, 2007; Kim and Bahry, 2008; Lehoucq, 2008; Hochstetler and Edwards, 2009; Llanos and Marsteintredet, 2010). Yet, whereas case studies of presidential downfalls often also invoke the dangers of presidents relying too heavily on their unilateral powers, existing quantitative analyses accord little role to the president's formal institutional powers. By contrast, this book shows that partisan status indeed matters, but that the effects are conditional on the distribution of formal institutional powers. In addition, the book provides an overarching theoretical framework for incorporating familiar insights about the deleterious effects of protests and scandals, as well as demonstrates that public support for institutions generally affects the overall cost–benefit calculus that helps to drive such crises.

The third and perhaps most novel feature of the book's argument is the claim that raising the stakes of the presidency not only destabilizes the executive, but can also trigger legislative and judicial crises. Drawing on a dynamic version of the core bargaining model used to explain presidential crises, I show how the inability of the legislative opposition to credibly commit to refrain from deploying their sanctioning powers may prompt presidents at risk to launch offensive strikes against legislatures and/or courts. This suggests a new twist to Guillermo O'Donnell's (1994) influential notion of delegative democracy such that presidents seek to assert control over other institutions not merely to prove their omnipotence, but rather precisely because they fear becoming impotent down the road. As I discuss in more detail below, arguing that crises are interconnected in this way also implicitly cuts against the current tendency to assume that presidential crises represent a uniformly positive turn in the institutional evolution of Latin America's democracies whereby legislatures are gaining a kind of newfound supremacy (cf. Pérez-Liñán, 2005; Marsteintredet and Berntzen, 2008).

7.2 IMPLICATIONS AND EXTENSIONS

The central focus of this book has been on developing a micro-level theory of the origins of inter-branch crises and then exploring how well it accounts for empirical patterns of institutional crises across the three major branches of government. My main goal has been to elucidate the conditions that lead bargaining to fail among political actors, as opposed to outlining a new normative theory about how inter-branch relations should operate or cataloguing the consequences of such failures. Of course, readers will have noticed that the discussion throughout has hardly been neutral; after all, nouns such as "crisis" and verbs such as "fail" clearly imply that something negative is afoot. At the outset of the book, the justification for such pessimism rested on two key observations: (1) despite politicians' rhetoric and their ability to invoke the mantle of constitutionalism, in practice, most sanctions are used opportunistically; and (2) even if this is not always the case, according to standard theories of checks and balances, sanctions should function mainly as a deterrent. That we routinely saw sanctions being deployed strongly suggested that institutions in contemporary Latin America are not functioning optimally. And yet, experts – at least those who focus on presidential crises – have often reached far more optimistic conclusions. The question taken up here is what lessons the analysis in the book holds for larger practical and normative debates about the consequences of institutional instability.

7.2.1 Legislative Supremacy

Let me start with claims about legislative supremacy. When unpopular or ineffective executives are removed before their terms are completed, scholars have touted presidential systems for developing quasi-parliamentary procedures (Carey, 2005; Pérez- Liñán, 2005; Hochstetler, 2006; Marsteintredet and Berntzen, 2008; Hochstetler and Samuels, 2011). And as legislatures exercise more power over executives, their logic goes, horizontal and vertical accountability soars. "In country after country," Marsteintredet and Berntzen write, "congress prevails if there is a conflict with the president, thus reducing somewhat the perils related to dual legitimacy, and popular strikes and protests show that the people can shortcut the fixed terms associated with presidents" (2008: 97). Tempting as such optimism is, the book shows that when we take all three branches into account, the verdict is far less clear. Two patterns from Chapter 2 stand out. First, Latin American presidents have, in fact, been nearly as aggressive as legislatures in initiating crises. Second, though presidents have tended to target courts more than they have targeted Congress, whenever they pick fights with either branch, they tend to win. By contrast, legislatures issue more threats against presidents and fewer against courts, but both types rarely succeed.

7.2.2 Spillover versus Substitution

A related lesson of the book that cuts against more optimistic assessments is that one type of institutional instability does not necessarily substitute for another. Latin American democratic regimes may indeed now be relatively stable in the midst of such crises, but presidential crises do not only affect presidents. Rather, Chapters 5 and 6 have provided both anecdotal and systematic evidence that presidents who were at risk of removal were significantly more likely to try to gain control over their legislatures and/ or courts. Likewise, I discovered that legislative attacks on courts were themselves partly reactive; that is, they were influenced by the current executive's efforts to seize control over the judiciary. Taken together, this hints at a chain of consequences in which the prospect of presidential crises serves as kind of tripwire that provokes presidents at risk to target the legislature and/or courts. To the extent that presidents succeed in remaking courts in their own image, this then potentially sets off a second wave of judicial crises by legislators bent on undoing the president's efforts.

7.2.3 Instability Traps or Inoculation?

In addition, the book also points to another type of spillover effect in which certain types of crises are prone to repeat within particular countries – witness the decade-long patterns of presidential ousters in Ecuador or judicial crises in Argentina. In general, this book has treated such instances of repetition as independent events: because each of the presidents who served in Ecuador between 1997 and 2005 essentially confronted a similar toxic institutional environment in which extremely powerful constitutional powers combined with little to no partisan powers, it is entirely plausible that any repetition of presidential crises within countries is adequately explained by the basic observation that like conditions tend to produce like outcomes.[2]

But this may not be the entire story. An obvious extension of the book's main argument is that institutional crises that occur at time t can potentially alter endogenously the salient conditions that confront actors at time t + 1. Importantly, such shifts can either reinforce the tendency toward crises or undermine it. Extending the argument in this way recalls the approach to endogenous institutional change described by Greif and Laitin (2004). In their language, we might think of public opinion, or d in the model, partisan opposition, or p in the model, and the allocation of formal powers, or Q, as "quasi-parameters," which shift in the wake of a given crisis, thus making subsequent crises more or less likely. Consider the following two quotes by commentators on recent events in Guatemala and Brazil, respectively:

"Mr. Pérez Molina, 64, is the first president in Guatemalan history to resign over a corruption scandal, experts said, a striking rarity in a country long known for the impunity of its political establishment. And though the economy in Guatemala has lagged compared with those of other countries in Latin America, Mr. Pérez Molina's sudden reversal of fortune put it firmly within a wave of efforts elsewhere in the region to make political systems more accountable."[3]

"This is a coup, a traumatic injury to Brazil's presidential system," said Pedro Arruda, a political analyst at the Pontifical Catholic University in São Paulo. "This is just pretext to take down a president who was elected by 54 million people. She doesn't have foreign bank accounts, and she hasn't been accused of corruption, unlike those who are trying to impeach her ... It's putting a very large bullet in Brazilian democracy," said Lincoln Secco, a professor of history at the University of São Paulo. "This will set a very dangerous precedent for democracy in Brazil, because from now on, any moment that we have a highly unpopular president, there will be pressure to start an impeachment process."[4]

---

[2] Elkins and Simmons note that the logic of similar conditions producing similar outcomes informs most baseline models in comparative politics (200t5: 34–35). In his discussion of the third wave democratizations, Huntington refers to this sort of argument as parallel development, whereby independent events cluster temporally, but are otherwise causally unrelated (1991: 32).

[3] Ahmed and Malkin, "Otto Perez Molina of Guatemala Is Jailed Hours after Resigning Presidency," *New York Times*, September 3, 2015.

[4] Moura Jacobs and Sreeharsha, "Vote to Impeach Brazil's Leader Passes Strongly," *New York Times*, April 18, 2016.

Clearly, the views expressed above about the effects of presidential crises could not be more different. The former is optimistic. Inter-branch crises are salutary; they not only cleanse the system of corruption, but they set the country on a new path in which horizontal accountability can finally emerge. In a word, instability inoculates. By contrast, the second narrative, captured in the quote on the impeachment debacle in Brazil, forebodes a very different future. In this view, not only is the act of impeachment seen as unjust and undemocratic – overturning the votes of 54 million Brazilians – but the long-term consequences are feared to be even more pernicious. Politicians and citizens indeed learn from institutional crises, but they absorb a very different lesson. Thus, contrary to the instability qua inoculation mechanism, the implication here is that instability becomes a trap.

Building on the core bargaining model presented in this book offers a systematic framework for beginning to understand how either path might emerge. Let me start with the optimistic view. Recall that in the model sketched out in Chapter 3, presidents' best response to legislatures that have the incentive to oust them ($p - d > Q$) was to simply adjust their offer to E'. To the extent that a previous crisis helps subsequent presidents better understand precisely where E' lies, bargains can now be struck. Likewise, to the extent that the credibility of legislators and judges is enhanced by the crisis, the costs to the next president for launching preventive strikes against these institutional actors rise accordingly. Implicitly, this is similar to the positive dynamic suggested in North and Weingast's foundational work on the Glorious Revolution (1989; see also Weingast 1997). By their interpretation, the king was beheaded for trampling rights, and thereafter leaders and citizens alike learned the limits of the government.

Conversely, however, the main payoffs might instead change in ways that makes subsequent crises more likely. Starting with p, which again is the probability that the opposition succeeds in removing the president, if a previous crisis teaches leaders how to reign in their power, it also teaches opposition politicians how to coordinate to effectively remove presidents; thus, E' becomes a moving target. Likewise, if crises destroy trust in institutions, not just particular leaders (i.e., a lower d in the next rounds), then this lowers the threshold for presidential crises going forward. Put differently, if crises serve to both endogenously lower the legislature's threshold for removal by raising p and reducing d, then crises become that much more likely down the road.

Last but not least, the model also reminds us of the importance of changing the formal institutions that allocate presidential power in the wake of the crisis. If the theory is right, one of the most disheartening facts about a country like Ecuador is that, in the wake of such crises, incoming presidents have falsely inferred that strengthening the president's constitutional powers will help them overcome any weaknesses associated with being in the minority. Instead, the model tells us that reforms that push Q to the left will only exacerbate inter-branch bargaining failures. Along these very lines, Mejía Acosta and Polga-Hecimovich (2010) highlight the perverse consequences of granting the president more unilateral powers in periods following Durán-Ballén's troubled administration. In particular, they describe how such reforms increased the president's incentives to go it alone and reduced the president's capacity to forge lasting coalitions, thus resulting in the wave of repeated presidential ousters post-1996.

7.2.4 The Effects of Inter-Branch Crises on Trust and the Economy

To be sure, we can never know ex ante which type of cycle will prevail for a particular country, but with a strong theoretical framework in place, we at least know where to begin to look. If public support for institutions crumbles, and/or leaders reform institutions in such a way that raises the stakes for the opposition being out of power, then the theory suggests that the country will be that much more prone to an instability trap. Conversely, if such crises build trust or help close the gap in presidential power, then perhaps optimism is justified. Empirically, an obvious area for future research is thus to establish the nature and duration of the various effects of each type of crisis. Along these lines, Hochstetler and Samuels (2011) analyze a slew of governance and economic indicators and find limited evidence that presidential crises in Latin America have lasting effects. Yet the debate has only begun.

Expanding beyond presidential crises, I begin with a cursory look at the effects of different types of crises on public trust in institutions using data from the Latinobarómetro. Specifically, I consider how the initiation of each of the four types of inter-branch crises (i.e., presidential crises, legislative crises, and judicial crises instigated by the president or the legislature) affects public trust in institutions in the subsequent year, controlling for public trust in the previous year. Figure 7.1 reports the results for each of the eight simple models. The four arrows indicate the particular ordered dyad involved in the crisis. For each arrow, there are two coefficients reported for each dyadic actor that represent the impact

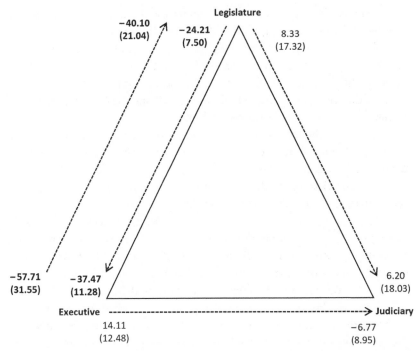

FIGURE 7.1: Effects of inter-branch crises on public support.

on public trust at $t + 1$ as a function of the crisis at t, controlling for public trust in that institution at t. The coefficients that are significant appear in bold.[5]

Although the analysis here is obviously quite provisional, the results suggest that both presidential and legislative crises take an immediate toll on the elected branches, whereas judicial crises do not. Moreover, these effects occur whether the attack succeeds or fails, suggesting that institutional crises are enormously costly, at least in the short run, regardless of whether or not unpopular politicians stay or go. The significant negative effects on the legislature and executive also remain whether we cluster the standard errors or run fixed effects models at the country level. Interestingly, however, using a fixed effects model (not shown here) reveals that within countries presidents actually gain roughly 24 points in their popularity through judicial manipulation, but this is the only type

---

[5] Significance is calculated at the 10 percent level.

of instability that correlates with support for the aggressor branch. On average then, presidential and legislative instability appear to make both branches more vulnerable, whereas judicial manipulation actually helps to shore up presidents. Moreover, the fact that presidents are arguably far more sensitive than legislators to a decline in public trust may give us some additional insight into why both judicial and presidential crises tend to repeat, whereas legislative crises do not.

What about the effects of inter-branch crises on the economy? Here, as above, problems of endogeneity and omitted variables limit our ability to draw definitive conclusions. However, preliminary work by Gibilisco and Helmke (2013) suggests that institutional crises do matter for the economy, at least in the short run. They find, for instance, not only that a presidential crisis is correlated with 1 to 2 percent lower growth in the subsequent year, but that the mere prospect of presidential instability hurts the economy by as much as 7 percent.[6] Interestingly, however, they show that most of these effects are confined to presidential crises involving leaders on the left. In line with the original business cycle theory pioneered by Hibbs (1977), which posits that leftist parties produce higher growth rates than their conservative counterparts, they find that the economic growth is hindered only when leftist presidents are attacked. Future work should thus continue to draw on the rich store of existing theories of political economy to guide our exploration of the effects not only of presidential crises, but also crises involving legislatures and courts. To give one example, the data on judicial instability can be further exploited to investigate anew the purported relationship between attacks on the rule of law and investment (cf. North and Weingast 1989)

7.3 INSTITUTIONAL REFORM: SOLUTIONS AND TRADE-OFFS

For those who believe that institutional instability is inherently problematic, the implications for institutional reform that come out of the book's main argument are clear enough. At least at first glance, the obvious solution is to narrow the gap between the president's constitutional powers and partisan powers. This can be accomplished in one of two ways: either by reducing the president's formal legislative powers and/or by increasing their seat share in the legislature. Neither solution is particularly novel, nor especially easy.

---

[6] To calculate this effect they use a forecasting model in which the first stage replicates the core statistical model used in Chapter 4 to predict presidential crises.

Scholars of presidentialism – albeit for reasons more associated with regime instability than institutional instability – have long called for a reduction of the president's de jure powers. Two decades have passed since Shugart and Carey first made their cogent argument that presidentialist systems stand a much better chance of regulating conflict if the president's legislative powers are "carefully circumscribed" (1992: 286), but real-world examples of reforms that effectively limit presidential powers are hard to find. In fact, the trend in constitutional reform in Latin America appears to have headed in exactly the opposite direction. Keeping with the observation that presidents will push to expand their legislative powers, in countries such as Argentina, Ecuador, Peru, and Venezuela, constituent assemblies dominated by the president's supporters have made presidents only more powerful (Negretto 2014: 261–262).

What is more, even if presidential powers could be ratcheted down, this hardly solves all of the problems associated with presidentialism. Under a scenario of divided government, gridlock still remains a very real possibility unless presidents have no reactive powers whatsoever. And to the extent that public expectations take time to catch up to institutional reforms, citizens may continue to expect presidents to be stronger than they are, blaming them when they fail to solve the nation's problems (O'Donnell, 1994). In the extreme, presidents would thus still remain vulnerable to the "street." A few bouts of this sort of instability later and citizens and politicians alike might well be clamoring to make presidents more powerful than ever.

What about increasing the president's partisan powers, then? Certainly, it is difficult to find any serious scholar of Latin American institutions who has not acknowledged the dangers associated with minority government, or pondered various ways to reduce the fragmentation of party systems. Whether moving to a concurrent electoral cycle, lowering district magnitude, adopting plurality versus proportional representation, and/or avoiding presidential run-off elections, there is no shortage of policy recommendations for how to go about lowering the effective number of parties. And surely, in terms of the arguments made in this book, any reforms that bolster a president's chances of earning a legislative majority would seem to go a long way toward reducing the legislature's incentives for attacking the president and vice versa.

Yet, here too, the solution is quite not as simple, or as foolproof, as it sounds. First, building stable party systems of any sort still remains frustratingly elusive, at least for many Latin American countries. Second, careful readers will note that reforms that bring about legislative majorities will not necessarily reduce all forms of institutional instability. Recall the point made in Chapter 6 that while the president's incentives to attack the courts may be reduced under majority governments, the president's capacity to get rid of any opposition hold over judges obviously increases with the proportion of seats they control in Congress.

Other objections revolve around what could potentially happen if the effective number of parties is reduced. On the one hand, if the president still does not achieve a majority, then fewer parties may simply mean that the president now confronts a more unified opposition. In line with the points made in Chapter 4, one could suppose that just as it is easier for minority presidents to build legislative coalitions when parties are less fragmented, presumably it is also easier for presidential opponents to craft impeachment coalitions when there are fewer parties. To be sure, if fewer opposition parties increase the credibility of legislative threats, then this may help presidents overcome any information asymmetries, thus allowing them to adjust their behavior and avoid sanctions. Alternatively, however, it may instead mean that presidents are merely at greater risk, thus actually raising the likelihood of the consequent patterns of instability that we have identified.

On the other hand, assuming that any electoral reforms did succeed in increasing the president's partisan powers and we are back in a world where presidential and legislative institutions are in accord, other concerns quickly crop up. For scholars of presidentialism, the downside of having all-powerful, Westminster-style presidents is well-covered territory. Most obviously, constraints on the executive branch potentially suffer. Recalling the basic impeachment game proposed in Chapter 1, the danger now becomes presidents breaking the law and get away with it (outcome B), not sanctions failing to deter presidents from breaking the law and being implemented (outcome A). Moreover, depending on the particular recipe of electoral reforms, the other risk in limiting the number of parties in the legislature is that fewer citizens may be represented (Powell, 2000). Thus, the real cost of institutional stability may be not the lack of flexibility, but a decline in political responsiveness. and good governance.

Unfortunately, offsetting unified governments by imbuing other institutions such as courts or other public agencies with the power to impose greater horizontal accountability risks failure at the outset, or just recreates the potential for institutional instability that is displaced onto judges or other ostensibly "neutral" actors. After all, majority presidents have little trouble quashing judicial independence. Thus, any separation of powers theorist would readily tell us that judges operating under this scenario will either adjust their behavior accordingly (i.e., go along with the government) or pay the consequences. Moreover, if the underlying logic of this book is correct, then the more power these sorts of institutions have, the more attractive a target they become for politicians to try to control.[7]

In the end, there are no magic bullets, just trade-offs. Decreasing presidential powers through constitutional reform is obviously difficult, and, if presidents were to remain in the minority, but still expected to lead the nation, then the challenges associated with divided government may ultimately convince actors that the cure is worse than the disease. Likewise, reducing the effective number of parties may also prove to be a double-edged sword. Either presidents would still remain in the minority and potentially confront a more coherent opposition or they would become majoritarian leaders, but then opportunities for representation and checks and balances could suffer. Precisely because institutional stability cannot easily be engineered, or may come at a price that we do not wish to pay, the sorts of crises that this book has focused on are likely to persist. Thus, understanding why, when, where, and how crises emerge is imperative for understanding contemporary politics both in Latin America and in other developing presidential systems around the world.

---

[7] Although provisional analysis has revealed no correlation between formal measures of judicial independence and judicial instability (Helmke and Ríos-Figueroa, 2011), this could well be due to the fact that most of the time judges are rightly reluctant to push their de jure powers beyond what their de facto environments will bear.

Bibliography

Acosta, Andrés Mejía, and John Polga-Hecimovich. 2010. Parliamentary Solutions to Presidential Crises in Ecuador. In *Presidential Breakdowns in Latin America: Causes and Outcomes of Executive Instability in Developing Democracies*, ed. Mariana Llanos and Leiv Marsteintredet. New York: Palgrave Macmillan.

Alemán, Eduardo, and George Tsebelis. 2005. "Presidents, Parties and Agenda Control in Latin America." Working paper.

Álvarez, Michael E., and Leiv Marsteintredet. 2009. Presidential and Democratic Breakdowns in Latin America: Similar Causes, Different Outcomes. In *Presidential Breakdowns in Latin America: Causes and Outcomes of Executive Instability in Developing Democracies*, ed. Mariana Llanos and Leiv Marsteintredet. New York: Palgrave Macmillan.

Anderson, Leslie E., and Lawrence C. Dodd. 2009. "Nicaragua: Progress amid Regress?" *Journal of Democracy* 20(3): 153–167.

Archer, Ron, and Matthew Shugart. 1997. The Unrealized Potential of Presidential Dominance in Colombia. In *Presidentialism and Democracy in Latin America*, ed. Scott Mainwaring and Matthew Shugart. New York: Cambridge University Press, pp. 110–159.

Baglini, Raúl, and Ángel D'Ambrosio. 1993. *Juicio a la Corte*. Buenos Aires: Mecanografix.

Banks, Arthur. 2005. *Cross-National Time-Series Data Archive*. Electronic format. Binghamton: State University of New York, Center for Social Analysis.

Basabe, Santiago, and John Polga-Hecimovich. 2013. "Legislative Coalitions and Judicial Turnover under Political Uncertainty: The Case of Ecuador." *Political Research Quarterly* 66(1): 153–165.

Bates, Robert H., Avner Greif, Margaret Levi, Jean-Laurent Rosenthal, and Barry R. Weingast. 1998. *Analytic Narratives*. Princeton, NJ: Princeton University Press.

Bjune, Maren Christensen, and Stina Petersen. 2010. Guarding Privileges and Saving the Day: Guatemalan Elites and the Settlement of the Serranazo. In *Presidential Breakdowns in Latin America*, ed. Mariana Llanos and Leiv Marsteintredet. New York: Palgrave Macmillan.

Boix, Carles. 1999. "Setting the Rules of the Game: The Choice of Electoral Systems in Advanced Democracies." *American Political Science Review*, 609–624.

Brambor, Thomas, William Clark, and Matt Golder. 2006. "Understanding Interaction Models: Improving Empirical Analyses." *Political Analysis* 14: 63–82.

Brewer-Carías, Allan. 2010. *Dismantling Democracy in Venezuela: The Chávez Authoritarian Experiment*. New York: Cambridge University Press.

Bueno De Mesquita, Bruce, and David Lalman. 1994. *War and Reason: Domestic and International Imperatives*. New Haven, CT: Yale University Press.

Buitrago, Miguel A. 2010. Civil Society, Social Protest, and Presidential Break-downs in Bolivia. In *Presidential Breakdowns in Latin America*, ed. Mariana Llanos and Leiv Marsteintredet. New York: Palgrave Macmillan.

Caldeira, Gregory A. 1986. "Neither the Purse nor the Sword: Dynamics of Public Confidence in the Supreme Court." *American Political Science Review*, 1209–1226.

Cameron, Charles M. 2000. *Veto Bargaining: Presidents and the Politics of Negative Power*. Cambridge: Cambridge University Press.

Cameron, Maxwell A. 1998. "Self-Coups: Peru, Guatemala, and Russia." *Journal of Democracy* 9(1): 125–139.

Carey, John. 2003. Presidentialism and Representative Institutions. In *Constructing Democratic Governance in Latin America*, ed. Jorge Dominguez and Michael Shifter. Baltimore, MD: Johns Hopkins University Press.

Carey, John M. 2005. Presidential versus Parliamentary Government. In *Handbook of New Institutional Economics*, ed. Claude Menard and Mary M. Shirley. Dordrecht: Springer.

2009. "Palace Intrigue: Missiles, Treason, and the Rule of Law in Bolivia." *Perspectives on Politics* 7(2): 351–356.

Carey, John M., and Matthew Soberg Shugart. 1998. *Executive Decree Authority*. Cambridge: Cambridge University Press.

Carrubba, Clifford J. 2009. "A Model of the Endogenous Development of Judicial Institutions in Federal and International Systems." *Journal of Politics*, 71(1): 1–15.

Castagnola, Andrea, and Aníbal Pérez-Liñán. 2011. Bolivia: The Rise (and Fall) of Judicial Review. In *Courts in Latin America*, ed. Gretchen Helmke and Julio Ríos-Figueroa. Cambridge: Cambridge University Press.

Chávez, Rebecca Bill, John A. Ferejohn, and Barry R. Weingast. 2011. *A Theory of the Politically Independent Judiciary: A Comparative Study of the United States and Argentina*. New York: Cambridge University Press.

Cheibub, José A. 2002. "Minority Governments, Deadlock Situations, and the Survival of Presidential Democracies." *Comparative Political Studies* 35(3): 284–312.

Cheibub, José Antonio. 2007. *Presidentialism, Parliamentarism, and Democracy.* Cambridge: Cambridge University Press.

Clarke, Kevin A., and David M. Primo. 2012. *A Model Discipline: Political Science and the Logic of Representations.* Oxford: Oxford University Press.

Conaghan, Catherine M. 2008. "Ecuador: Correa's Plebiscitary Presidency." *Journal of Democracy* 19(2): 46–60.

Coppedge, Michael. 1996. The Rise and Fall of Partyarchy in Venezuela. In *Constructing Democratic Governance: Latin America and the Caribbean in the 1990s,* ed. Jorge Dominguez and Abraham F. Lowenthal. Baltimore, MD: Johns Hopkins University Press, pp. 3–19.

Coppedge, Michael. 2003. Venezuela: Popular Sovereignty versus Liberal Democracy. In *Constructing Democratic Governance,* ed. Domínguez and Shifter.

Cox, Gary. 1997. *Making Votes Count: Strategic Coordination in the World's Electoral Systems.* Cambridge: Cambridge University Press.

Cox, Gary W., and Scott Morgenstern. 2002. Epilogue: Latin Americas Reactive Assemblies and Proactive Presidents. In *Legislative Politics in Latin America,* ed. Scott Morgenstern and Benito Nacif. Cambridge: Cambridge University Press.

de la Torre, Carlos. N.d. "Rafael Correa un Populista del Siglo XXI." Working paper.

Diamond, Larry, and Juan J. Linz. 1989. Introduction: Politics, Society, and Democracy in Latin America. In *Democracy in Developing Countries: Latin America,* ed. Larry Diamond, Juan J. Linz, and Seymour Martin Lipset. Boulder, CO: Lynne Rienner.

Domínguez, Jorge I., and Michael Shifter. 2003. *Constructing Democratic Governance in Latin America.* Baltimore, MD: Johns Hopkins University Press.

Duverger, Maurice. 1954. *Political Parties: Their Organization and Activity in the Modern State.* Taylor & Francis.

Elkins, Zachary, and Beth Simmons. 2005. "On Waves, Clusters, and Diffusion: A Conceptual Framework." *Annals of the American Academy of Political and Social Science* 598: 33–51.

Ellner, Steve. 2003. Introduction: The Search for Explanations. In *Venezuelan Politics in the Chávez Era: Class, Polarization and Conflict,* ed. Steve Ellner and Daniel Hellinger. London: Lynne Rienner.

Epstein, Lee, and Jack Knight. 1998. *The Choices Justices Make.* Washington, DC: Congressional Quarterly.

Fearon, James D. 1995. "Rationalist Explanations for War." *International Organization.* 49: 379–414.

1998. Commitment Problems and the Spread of Ethnic Conflict. In *The International Spread of Ethnic Conflict.* Princeton, NJ: Princeton University Press, pp. 107–126.

2004. "Why Do Some Civil Wars Last So Much Longer Than Others?" *Journal of Peace Research* 41(3): 275–301.

Ferejohn, John A., and Barry R. Weingast. 1992. "A Positive Theory of Statutory Interpretation." *International Review of Law and Economics* 12(2): 263–279.

Ferreira Rubio, Delia, and Matteo Goretti. 1998. When the President Governs Alone: The *Decretazo* in Argentina, 1989–1993. In *Executive Decree*

Authority, ed. John M. Carey and Matthew Soberg Shugart. Cambridge: Cambridge University Press.

Few, Mark, and Kris W. Ramsay. 2011. "Uncertainty and Incentives in Crisis Bargaining: Game-Free Analysis of International Conflict." *American Journal of Political Science.*

Fey, Mark, and Kristopher W. Ramsay. 2006. "The Common Priors Assumption." *Journal of Conflict Resolution* 50(4): 607–613.

Filson, Darren, and Suzanne Werner. 2002. "A Bargaining Model of War and Peace: Anticipating the Onset, Duration, and Outcome of War." *American Journal of Political Science*, 819–837.

Finkel, Jodi S. 2008. *Judicial Reform as Political Insurance: Argentina, Peru, and Mexico in the 1990s.* Notre Dame, IN: University of Notre Dame Press.

Fish, Steven. 2009. Stronger Legislatures, Stronger Democracies. In *Democracy: A Reader*, ed. Larry Diamond and Marc F. Plattner. Baltimore, MD: Johns Hopkins University Press, pp. 196–210.

Flynn, Peter. 1993. "Collor, Corruption and Crisis: Time for Reflection." *Journal of Latin American Studies* 25: 351–371.

Friedman, Barry E. 2009. *The Will of the People: How Public Opinion Has Influenced the Supreme Court and Shaped the Meaning of the Constitution.* New York: Farrar, Straus and Giroux.

Fujimori, Alberto. 2009. Manifesto a la Nación del 5 de Abril de 1992. In *Proceso de retorno a la institucionalidad democrática en el Perú*, ed. Larry Diamond and Marc F. Plattner. Baltimore, MD: Johns Hopkins University Press, pp. 196–210.

Fundación para el Debido Proceso Legal. 2010. "Independencia Judicial en Venezuela."

García-Serra, Mario J. 2001. "The 'Enabling Law': The Demise of the Separation of Powers in Hugo Chávez's Venezuela." *University of Miami Inter American Law Review* 3(2): 265–293.

Gely, Rafael, and Pablo T. Spiller. 1990. "A Rational Choice Theory of Supreme Court Statutory Decisions with Applications to the *State Farm* and *Grove City Cases*." *Journal of Law, Economics, & Organization* 6(2): 263–300.

Gibilisco, Michael, and Gretchen Helmke. 2013. "The Economic Effects of Executive Instability in Latin America." Working paper.

Ginsburg, Tom. 2003. *Judicial Review in New Democracies: Constitutional Courts in Asian Cases.* Cambridge: Cambridge University Press.

Greif, Avner, and David D. Laitin. 2004. "A Theory of Endogenous Institutional Change." *American Political Science Review* 98(4): 633–652.

Grijalva, Agustín, and Aníbal Pérez-Liñán. 2003. "Presidential Powers Database." Department of Political Science, University of Pittsburgh (computer file).

Hagopian, Frances, and Scott P. Mainwaring. 2005. *The Third Wave of Democratization in Latin America: Advances and Setbacks.* Cambridge: Cambridge University Press.

Hamilton, Alexander, James Madison, and John Jay. 1961 [1788]. *The Federalist Papers.* New York: New American Library.

Hammergren, L. 2007. *Envisioning Reform: Conceptual and Practical Obstacles to Improving Judicial Performance in Latin America.* University Park: Pennsylvania State University Press.

Harvey, Anna, and Barry Friedman. 2006. "Pulling Punches: Congressional Constraints on the Supreme Court's Constitutional Rulings, 1987–2000." *Legislative Studies Quarterly* 31(4): 533–562.

Hellwig, Timothy, and David Samuels. 2007. "Voting in Open Economies." *Comparative Political Studies* 40(3): 283–306.

Helmke, Gretchen. 2002. "The Logic of Strategic Defection: Court–Executive Relations in Argentina under Dictatorship and Democracy." *American Political Science Review* 96(2): 291–303.

2005. *Courts under Constraints: Judges, Generals, and Presidents in Argentina.* New York: Cambridge University Press.

2010. "The Origins of the Institutional Crises in Latin America." *American Journal of Political Science* 54(3): 737–750.

2016. "Introducing the Leaders on Trial Dataset for Post-War Latin America." Working paper.

Helmke, Gretchen, and Julio Ríos-Figueroa. 2011. *Introduction: Courts in Latin America.* New York: Cambridge University Press.

Helmke, Gretchen, and Frances Rosenbluth. 2009. "Regimes and the Rule of Law: Judicial Independence in Comparative Perspective." *Annual Review of Political Science* 12: 345–366.

Helmke, Gretchen, and Jeffery Staton. 2010. *Judicial Power and Strategic Communication in Mexico.* New York: Cambridge University Press.

Herron, Erik S., and Kirk A. Randazzo. 2003. "The Relationship between Independence and Judicial Review in Post-Communist Courts." *Journal of Politics* 65(2): 422–438.

Hibbs, D. A. 1977. "Political Parties and Macroeconomic Policy." *American Political Science Review* 71(4): 1467–1487.

Hinojosa, Victor, and Aníbal Pérez-Liñán. 2003. Presidential Impeachment and the Politics of Survival: The Case of Colombia. In *Checking Executive Power: Presidential Impeachment in Comparative Perspective,* ed. Frances Hagopian and Scott Mainwaring. Westport, CT: Greenwood Press, pp. 65–79.

Hochstetler, Kathryn. 2006. "Rethinking Presidentialism: Challenges and Presidential Falls in South America." *Comparative Politics* 38(4): 401–418.

Hochstetler, Kathryn, and Margaret E. Edwards. 2009. "Failed Presidencies: Identifying and Explaining a South American Anomaly." *Journal of Politics in Latin America* 1(2): 31–57.

Hochstetler, Kathryn, and David Samuels. 2011. "Crisis and Rapid Reequilibration: The Consequences of Presidential Challenge and Failure in Latin America." *Comparative Politics* 43(2): 127–145.

Huntington, S. P. 1991. "Democracy's Third Wave." *Journal of Democracy* 2(2): 12–34.

Jonas, Susanne. 1994. "Text and Subtext of the Guatemalan Political Drama." *LASA Forum* 24(4): 3–9.

Jones, Mark P. 1995. *Electoral Laws and the Survival of Presidential Democracies.* Notre Dame, IN: University of Notre Dame Press.

1997. *Evaluating Argentina's Presidential Democracy: 1983–1995.* Cambridge: Cambridge University Press, pp. 259–299.

Kada, Naoko. 2003. Impeachment as a Punishment for Corruption? The Cases of Brazil and Venezuela. In *Checking Executive Power: Presidential Impeachment in Comparative Perspective*, ed. Jody C. Baumgartner and Naoko Kada. Westport, CT: Praeger, pp. 113–136.

Kahneman, Daniel, Paul Slovic, and Amos Tversky. 1982. *Judgment under Uncertainty: Heuristics and Biases.* Cambridge: Cambridge University Press.

Kenney, Charles D. 2004. *Fujimori's Coup and the Breakdown of Democracy in Latin America.* Notre Dame, IN: University of Notre Dame Press.

Kim, Youngh Hun, and Donna Bahry. 2008. "Interrupted Presidencies in Third Wave Democracies." *Journal of Politics* 70(3): 807–822.

King, Gary, and Langche Zeng. 2001. "Logistic Regression in Rare Events Data." *Political Analysis* 9(2): 137–163.

Knight, Jack. 1992. *Institutions and Social Conflict.* Cambridge: Cambridge University Press.

La Porta, Rafael, Florencio López de Silanes, Cristian Pop-Eleches, and Andrei Shleifer. 2004. "Judicial Checks and Balances." *Journal of Political Economy* 112: 445–470.

Lalander, Rickard. 2010. The Impeachment of Carlos Andrés Pérez and the Collapse of Venezuelan Partyarchy. In *Presidential Breakdowns in Latin America: Causes and Outcomes of Executive Instability in Developing Democracies*, ed. Mariana Llanos and Leiv Marsteintredet. New York: Palgrave Macmillan.

Larkins, Christopher. 1998. "The Judiciary and Delegative Democracy in Argentina." *Comparative Politics*, 423–442.

Lehoucq, Fabrice. 2005. "Constitutional Design and Democratic Performance in Latin America." Available at http://lanic.utexas.edu/project/etext/llilas/vrp/lehoucq.pdf.

2008. "Bolivia's Constitutional Breakdown." *Journal of Democracy* 19(4): 110–124.

Levine, Daniel H. 2008. "The Logic of Bolivarian Democracy in Venezuela: Domestic and International Connections." Paper presented at the meeting of the American Political Science Association, Boston.

Levitsky, Steven. 2005. Argentina: Democratic Survival amidst Economic Failure. In *The Third Wave of Democratization in Latin America: Advances and Setbacks*, ed. Frances Hagopian and Scott P. Mainwaring. Cambridge: Cambridge University Press.

Levitsky, Steven, and Maxwell A. Cameron. 2003. "Democracy without Parties? Political Parties and Regime Change in Fujimori's Peru." *Latin American Politics and Society* 45(3): 1–33.

Linz, Juan J. 1990. "The Perils of Presidentialism." *Journal of Democracy* 1(1): 51–69.

1994. Democracy, Presidential or Parliamentary: Does It Make a Difference? In *The Failure of Presidential Democracy: The Case of Latin America*, ed. Juan J. Linz and Arturo Valenzuela. Baltimore, MD: Johns Hopkins University Press.

Llanos, Mariana, and Leiv Marsteintredet. 2010. Conclusions: Presidential Break-downs Revisited. In *Presidential Breakdowns in Latin America: Causes and Outcomes of Executive Instability in Developing Democracies*, ed. Mariana Llanos and Leiv Marsteintredet. New York: Palgrave Macmillan.

Londregan, John B., and Keith T. Poole. 1990. "Poverty, the Coup Trap, and the Seizure of Executive Power." *World Politics* 42(2): 151–183.

Magaloni, Beatriz. 2003. "Authoritarianism, Democracy and the Supreme Court: Horizontal Exchange and the Rule of Law in Mexico," pp. 266–305.

Mainwaring, Scott P. 1993. "Presidentialism, Multipartism, and Democracy: The Difficult Combination." *Comparative Political Studies* 26(2): 198–228.

2006. "The Crisis of Representation in the Andes." *Journal of Democracy* 17 (3): 13–27.

2014. *Democracies and Dictatorships in Latin America: Emergence, Survival, and Fall*. New York: Cambridge University Press.

Mainwaring, Scott, and Aníbal Pérez-Liñán. 2005. Latin American Democratiza-tion since 1978: Democratic Transitions, Breakdowns and Erosions. In *The Third Wave of Democratization in Latin America: Advances and Setbacks*, ed. Frances Hagopian and Scott Mainwaring. Cambridge: Cambridge University Press, pp. 14–59.

Mainwaring, Scott P., and Matthew S. Shugart. 1997. *Presidentialism and Democracy in Latin America*. Cambridge: Cambridge University Press.

Manin, Bernard. 1989. Checks, Balances and Boundaries: The Separation of Powers in the Constitutional Debate of 1787. In *The Invention of the Modern Republic*, ed. Biancamaria Fontana. Cambridge: Cambridge University Press.

Marcano, Cristina, and Alberto Barrera Tyszka. 2007. *Hugo Chávez*. New York: Random House.

Marsteintredet, Leiv. 2010. The Dominican Republic and the Fall of Balaguer 1994–1996: Presidential Breakdown or Democratic Transition? In *Presiden-tial Breakdowns in Latin America: Causes and Outcomes of Executive Instability in Developing Democracies*, ed. Mariana Llanos and Leiv Mar-steintrdet. New York: Palgrave Macmillan.

Marsteintredet, Leiv, and Einar Berntzen. 2008. "Reducing the Perils of Presiden-tialism in Latin America through Presidential Interruptions." *Comparative Politics* 41(1): 83–101.

McCleary, Rachel M. 1997. "Guatemala's Postwar Prospects." *Journal of Dem-ocracy* 8(2): 129–143.

McCoy, Jennifer. 1999. "Chávez and the End of Partyarchy in Venezuela." *Journal of Democracy* 10(3): 64–77.

McDonald, Ronald H., and J. Mark Ruhl. 1989. *Party Politics and Elections in Latin America*. Boulder, CO: Westview Press.

Mejía Acosta, Andres. 2006. Crafting Legislative Ghost Coalitions in Ecuador: Informal Institutions and Economic Reform in an Unlikely Case. In *Informal Institutions and Democracy: Lessons from Latin America*, ed. Gretchen Helmke and Steven Levitsky. Baltimore, MD: Johns Hopkins University Press.

2009. *Informal Coalitions and Policymaking in Latin America: Ecuador in Comparative Perspective*. New York: Routledge.

Mejía Acosta, Andres, and John Polga-Hecimovich. 2010. Parliamentary Solutions to Presidential Crises in Ecuador. In *Presidential Breakdowns in Latin America: Causes and Outcomes of Executive Instability in Developing Democracies*, ed. Mariana Llanos and Leiv Marsteintredet. New York: Palgrave Macmillan.

Morgenstern, Scott, and Benito Nacif, eds. 2002. *Legislative Politics in Latin America*. New York: Cambridge University Press.

Morgenstern, Scott, Juan Javier Negri, and Aníbal Pérez-Liñán. 2008. "Parliamentary Opposition in Non-Parliamentary Regimes: Latin America." *Journal of Legislative Studies* 14(1/2).

Mustapic, Ana María. 2010. Presidentialism and Early Exits: The Role of Congress. In *Presidential Breakdowns in Latin America: Causes and Outcomes of Executive Instability in Developing Democracies*, ed. Mariana Llanos and Leiv Marsteintredet. New York: Palgrave Macmillan.

Myers, David J. 2008. Delegate of Democracy or Electoral Autocracy? In *Constructing Democratic Governance in Latin America*, ed. Jorge I. Dominguez and Michael Shifter. Baltimore, MD: Johns Hopkins University Press.

Negretto, Gabriel L. 2004. "Government Capacities and Policy Making by Decree in Latin America: The Cases of Brazil and Argentina." *Comparative Political Studies* 37: 531–562.

2006. "Minority Presidents and Democratic Performance in Latin America." *Latin American Politics and Society* 48(3): 63–92.

2014. *Making Constitutions: Presidents, Parties, and Institutional Choice in Latin America*. New York: Cambridge University Press.

Nolte, Detlef. 2010. Paraguay: The President in His General's Labyrinth. In *Presidential Breakdowns in Latin America*, ed. Mariana Llanos and Leiv Marsteintredet. New York: Palgrave Macmillan.

North, Douglass C., and Barry R. Weingast. 1989. "Constitutions and Commitment: The Evolution of Institutions Governing Public Choice in Seventeenth Century England." *Journal of Economic History* 49(4): 803–832.

North, Douglass C., John Joseph Wallis, and Barry R. Weingast. 2009. *Violence and Social Orders*. New York: Cambridge University Press.

Octavio de Jesus, Marcelo, and Alejandra Ruscelli. 1998. "The Lasting Transition in the Judiciaries in South America: A Country Study." Presented at the XXI International Congress of the Latin American Studies Association, Chicago.

O'Donnell, Guillermo. 1994. "Delegative Democracy." *Journal of Democracy* 5(1): 55–69.

1999. *Counterpoints: Selected Essays on Authoritarianism and Democratization*. Notre Dame, IN: University of Notre Dame Press.

Olmsted, Jonathan, Curt Signorino, and Jun Xiang. 2015. "Aggregation Bias in Measures of Democracy." Working paper.

Pachano, Simón. 2007. "Ecuador: Two Years of Uncertainty." Working paper.

Pereira, Carlos, Timothy J. Power, and Lucio Renno. 2005. "Under What Conditions Do Presidents Resort to Decree Power? Theory and Evidence from the Brazilian Case." *Journal of Politics* 67(1): 178–200.

Pérez-Liñán, Aníbal. 2003. Presidential Crises and Political Accountability in Latin America, 1990–1999. In *What Justice? Whose Justice? Fighting for*

Bibliography 173

Fairness in Latin America, ed. Susan Eckstein and Timothy Wickham-Crowley. Berkeley: University of California Press, pp. 98–129.

2005. Latin American Democratization since 1978: Democratic Transition, Breakdowns and Erosions. In *The Third Wave of Democratization in Latin America: Advances and Setbacks*, ed. Frances Hagopian and Scott Mainwaring. Cambridge: Cambridge University Press, pp. 14–59.

2007. *Presidential Impeachment and the New Political Instability in Latin America*. New York: Cambridge University Press.

Pérez-Liñán, Aníbal, and Andrea Castagnola. 2014. "Judicial Instability and Endogenous Constitutional Change: Lessons from Latin America." *British Journal of Political Science* 46(2): 395–416.

Plattner, Marc F. 2010. "Populism, Pluralism, and Liberal Democracy." *Journal of Democracy* 21(1): 81–92.

Powell, G. Bingham. 2000. *Elections as Instruments of Democracy: Majoritarian and Proportional Visions*. New Haven, CT: Yale University Press.

Powell, Robert. 1999. *In the Shadow of Power: States and Strategies in International Politics*. Princeton, NJ: Princeton University Press.

2002. "Bargaining Theory and International Conflict." *Annual Review of Political Science* 5(1): 1–30.

2006. "War as a Commitment Problem." *International Organization* 60(1): 169.

Power, Manchego-Muñoz Jorge. 1989. El modelo constitucional del régimen político Peruano. In *La Constitución diez años después*. Lima: Fundación Friedrich Naumann, pp. 167–182.

Pozas-Loyo, Andrea, and Julio Ríos-Figueroa. 2010. "Enacting Constitutionalism: The Origins of Independent Judicial Institutions in Latin America." *Comparative Politics* 42(3): 293–311.

Przeworski, Adam. 1991. *Democracy and the Market: Political and Economic Reforms in Eastern Europe and Latin America*. Cambridge: Cambridge University Press.

Przeworski, Adam, Michael E. Alvarez, Jose Antonio Cheibub, and Fernando Limongi. 2000. *Democracy and Development: Political Institutions and Well-Being in the World, 1950–1990*. Cambridge: Cambridge University Press.

Rabin, Matthew. 1998. "Psychology and Economics." *Journal of Economic Literature* 36(1): 11–46.

Ramseyer, J. Mark. 1994. "The Puzzling (In)Dependence of Courts: A Comparative Approach." *The Journal of Legal Studies* 23(2): 721–747.

Ramseyer, J. Mark, and Eric Rasmusen. 1997. "Judicial Independence in a Civil Law Regime: The Evidence from Japan." *Journal of Law, Economics, and Organization* 13 (2): 259–287.

Ríos-Figueroa, Julio. 2011. Institutions for Constitutional Justice in Latin America. In *Courts in Latin America*, ed. Gretchen Helmke and Julio Ríos-Figueroa. New York: Cambridge University Press.

Rodríguez-Raga, Juan Carlos. 2011. Strategic Deference in the Colombian Constitutional Court: 1992–2006. In *Courts in Latin America*, ed. Gretchen Helmke and Julio Ríos-Figueroa. New York: Cambridge University Press.

Rodríguez Veltzé, Eduardo. 2001. Legal Security in Bolivia. In *Towards Democratic Viability: The Bolivian Experience*, ed. John Crabtree and Laurence Whitehead. New York: Palgrave, 179–194.

Rospigliosi, Fernando. 2000. *Montesinos y las fuerzas armadas: cómo controló durante una década las instituciones militares.* Vol. 14. Lima: Instituto de Estudios Peruanos.

Sánchez, Arianna, Beatriz Magaloni, and Eric Magar. 2011. Legalist versus Interpretativist: The Supreme Court and the Democratic Transition in Mexico. In *Courts in Latin America*, ed. Gretchen Helmke and Julio Ríos-Figueroa. Cambridge: Cambridge University Press.

Sanchez Urribarri, Raúl A. 2010. "Judges and Their Loyalties: A Comparative Study Focused on the Venezuelan Supreme Court." PhD dissertation, University of South Carolina.

Schamis, Hector E. 2006. "A 'Left Turn' in Latin America?: Populism, Socialism and Democratic Institutions." *Journal of Democracy* 17(4): 20–34.

Schelling, Thomas. 1960. *The Strategy of Conflict.* Cambridge, MA: Harvard University Press.

Schmidt, Gregory. 1998. Presidential Usurpation or Congressional Preference? The Evolution of Executive Decree Authority in Peru. In *Executive Decree Authority*, ed. John M. Carey and Matthew Sobery Shugart. New York: Cambridge University Press.

Seligson, Mitchell A. 2007. "The Rise of Populism and the Left in Latin America." *Journal of Democracy* 18(3): 81–95.

Shugart, Matthew S., and John M. Carey. 1992. *Presidents and Assemblies: Constitutional Design and Electoral Dynamics.* Cambridge: Cambridge University Press.

Siaroff, Alan. 2003. "Comparative Presidencies: The Inadequacy of the Presidential, Semi-Presidential and Parliamentary Distinction." *European Journal of Political Research* 42(3): 287–312.

Signorino, Curtis S. 1999. "Strategic Interaction and the Statistical Analysis of International Conflict." *American Political Science Review*, 279–297.

Signorino, Curtis S., and Kuzey Yilmaz. 2003. "Strategic Misspecification in Regression Models." *American Journal of Political Science* 47(3): 551–566.

Slantchev, B.L. 2003. "The Power to Hurt: Costly Conflict with Completely Informed States." *American Political Science Review* 97(1): 123–133.

Smith, Alastair, and Allan C. Stam. 2004. "Bargaining and the Nature of War." *Journal of Conflict Resolution* 48(6): 783–813.

2006. "Divergent Beliefs in 'Bargaining and the Nature of War.'" *Journal of Conflict Resolution* 50(4): 614–618.

Smulovitz, Catalina. 1995. "Constitución y poder judicial en la nueva democracia Argentina. La experiencia de las instituciones," pp. 71–114.

Staton, Jeffrey K. 2010. *Judicial Power and Strategic Communication in Mexico.* New York: Cambridge University Press.

Stokes, Susan C. 2001. *Mandates and Democracy: Neoliberalism by Surprise in Latin America.* Cambridge University Press.

Tanaka, Martín. 2005. Peru 1980–2000: Chronicle of a Death Foretold? Determinism, Political Decisions, and Open Outcomes. In *The Third Wave of Democratization in Latin America: Advances and Setbacks*, ed. Frances Hagopian and Scott P. Mainwaring. New York: Cambridge University Press.

Taylor, Matthew M. 2008. *Judging Policy: Courts and Policy Reform in Democratic Brazil*. Palo Alto, CA: Stanford University Press.

2009. "Curbing the Courts: A Model of Judicial Independence with Illustration from Chávez's Venezuela." Paper prepared for the annual meeting of the American Political Science Association, Toronto.

Toharia, José. 1975. "Judicial Independence in an Authoritarian Regime: The Case of Contemporary Spain." *Law and Society Review* 9 (Spring): 475–496.

Tomz, Michael, Gary King, and Langche Zeng. 2003. "ReLogit: Rare Events Logistic Regression." *Journal of Statistical Software* 8(2): 1–27.

Tsebelis, George. 2002. *Veto Players: How Political Institutions Work*. Princeton, NJ: Princeton University Press.

Valenzuela, Arturo. 2004. "Latin American Presidencies Interrupted." *Journal of Democracy* 15(4): 5–19.

Vanberg, Georg. 2005. *The Politics of Constitutional Review in Germany*. New York: Cambridge University Press.

Verbitsky, Horacio. 1993. *Hacer la corte: La construcción de un poder absoluto sin control ni justicia*. Buenos Aires: Planeta Buenos Aires.

Villagrán de León, Francisco. 1993. "Thwarting the Guatemalan Coup." *Journal of Democracy* 4(4): 117–124.

Wagner, R. Harrison. 2000. "Bargaining and War." *American Journal of Political Science*, 469–484.

Weingast, Barry R. 1997. "The Political Foundations of Democracy and the Rule of Law." *American Political Science Review*, pp. 245–263.

Weldon, Jeffrey. 1997. Political Sources of *Presidencialismo* in Mexico. In *Presidentialism and Democracy in Latin America*, ed. Scott P. Mainwaring and Matthew S. Shugart. Cambridge: Cambridge University Press, pp. 225–259.

Weyland, Kurt G. 1993. "The Rise and Fall of President Collor and Its Impact on Brazilian Democracy." *Journal of Interamerican Studies and World Affairs* 35(1): 1–37.

Learning from Foreign Models in Latin American Policy Reform. Washington, DC: Woodrow Wilson Center Press.

Wilpert, Gregory. 2007. *Changing Venezuela by Taking Power: The History and Policies of the Chávez Government*. New York: Verso.

Wittman, Donald. 2009. "Bargaining in the Shadow of War: When Is a Peaceful Resolution Most Likely?" *American Journal of Political Science* 53(3): 588–602.

Index